"In this time of great uncertainty, ever-increasing velocity of life and seemingly non-stop personal and social change, *Seekers: Finding Our Way Home* is a comforting rest stop as well as an important book. Paul Dunion is among the psychology field's most insightful theorists and practitioners today. In *Seekers*, Dunion shows us how to unplug from the confining places of modernity and live larger, more-embodied and meaningful lives."

—Thom Allena, Ph.D., Co-Author, *Restorative Justice on the College Campus: Promoting Student Growth and Responsibility, and Reawakening the Spirit of Campus Community*

"Paul Dunion is an educated, cultured, and thoughtful man. He writes here about how we move through our lives—the dynamics, the obstacles, the passages and the rewards. There's a fascinating toughness and grace in Paul's ideas and words. For me, he is a man of the twenty-first century, a guide for the soul's wilderness. This book speaks to the seeker in us all."

—Thomas Moore, author of *A Religion of One's Own*

"The life of a seeker is never easy. The journey *home* requires stretching beyond what's comfortable and is often filled with self-doubt, confusion, and loneliness. But the seeker has no choice but to seek, and in his latest book, author Paul Dunion explores what *home* is and how to have a deep, intimate relationship with life as we try to find our way there. He addresses how to live with meaning and wonder, the role of the aging seeker, and what to do when we lose our way. *Seekers* is an original, thought-provoking book written with Dr. Dunion's deep insights in a beautifully lyrical style."

—Jennifer Read Hawthorne, #1 New York Times bestselling coauthor, *Chicken Soup for the Woman's Soul*

"The essence of Dunion's book is the human imperative we all have to be seekers of beauty. To bring the gift of our living and meaning fully into our communities in a healing generative relationship with the earth. To be alive is to be seeking and nourishing the internal wilderness of one's soul, heart and love in life."

—Jeffery Duvall

SEEKERS

Finding Our Way Home

PAUL DUNION EdD

ARCHWAY
PUBLISHING

Archway Publishing books may be ordered through booksellers or by contacting:

Archway Publishing
1663 Liberty Drive
Bloomington, IN 47403
www.archwaypublishing.com
1 (888) 242-5904

Because of the dynamic nature of the Internet, any web addresses or links contained in this book may have changed since publication and may no longer be valid. The views expressed in this work are solely those of the author and do not necessarily reflect the views of the publisher, and the publisher hereby disclaims any responsibility for them.

Any people depicted in stock imagery provided by Thinkstock are models, and such images are being used for illustrative purposes only. Certain stock imagery © Thinkstock.

ISBN: 978-1-4808-3152-0 (sc)
ISBN: 978-1-4808-3153-7 (hc)
ISBN: 978-1-4808-3154-4 (e)

Library of Congress Control Number: 2016908247

Print information available on the last page.

Archway Publishing rev. date: 8/30/2016

Dedication

To the students of the Croton Mystery School for
their steadfast devotion as seekers. Their spirits bring
curiosity and wonder to the school's vision; their courage
and integrity create an inspired community.

Contents

Acknowledgments

I AM DEEPLY THANKFUL TO those who took the time to read and critically respond to rough drafts of my manuscript; Jennifer Jondreau Thompson, Margaret Harris, Jeffrey Duval, Thom Allena, Ray DiCapua, Liz Bochain, and Amy Dunion all added a great deal to the final product. I also continue to appreciate the support and faith in my writing offered by Thomas Moore.

I would not be able to draw upon my experience and intuition if it were not for the support and encouragement of old friends: Joanne Reeves, Gary Blaser, Michael Paprocki, Thom Allena, Clive West, Jeffrey Duval, Amy Dunion—and my old friend Norbert Gauthier, who stepped to the other side this past year. Each of them has in some way held me as I stepped onto unfamiliar internal terrain. When I found myself denying my limits and getting lost, they offered me a genuine welcome back home and blessed my efforts toward seeking.

I appreciate the collegiality I continue to share with Walter van Sambeck, who reminds me what it means to be a wounded healer. Thanks to Norcott Pemberton for calling me back to my humanity when I am inclined to shame some act of buffoonery. I am grateful to Vanessa Young and Heather Fessenden whose efforts moved the writing from my desk to its rightful place in the world. Many thanks to Jennifer Read Hawthorne, whose editorial touch brought the manuscript up to speed. I am deeply grateful to Ci Jones, an aging seeker, who offered some needed refinements to the last chapter.

At the end of the day, when self-doubt raises its voice, it is Connie Jones Dunion who holds me in her compassionate gaze. I linger there, with nothing to prove or demonstrate, and return to a rhythmic deep breath, releasing questions regarding my legitimacy. From that strengthening, I once again find the restlessness energizing my passion to seek.

Introduction

IF YOU HAVE READ ANY of my other books, you may have wondered: Why can't I simply get with the program and live like everyone else? Why am I not satisfied with the values and beliefs that everyone appears content with? Why does everyone else seem to be content with their answers, while I continue to have questions? Am I too idealistic? Am I suffering from some maladaptive syndrome?

These are often the kind of questions and doubts experienced by seekers. You too may be a seeker, and as such, you are a *threshold dweller*—someone who is familiar with the gateway from the familiar to the unknown. Your soul knows a restlessness calling you to somewhere beyond what is. You take great solace in stepping into a new vision of what life is about. You experience a strong call to know yourself better.

As a seeker, you share a deep kinship with the unknown, and you resist allowing your imagination to be domesticated. There is wildness in you, with a ferocity that releases you from taking up sanctuary in conventional wisdom. Such emancipation is fraught with challenges. Time and time again you will know self-doubt, confusion, and a deep sense of aloneness. Loved ones and friends will confront you about your alleged inability to accept things the way they are. Your visions will carry an idyllic seduction, calling you away from the ordinary.

You will need to learn to straddle both worlds—the one you are present to and the one you dream of. This is what this book aspires to help you accomplish.

What You'll Find in This Book

In this book you will find a large invitation either to affirm yourself as a seeker or to consider exploring what it means to seek. Seekers seek home. In Chapter 1, "The Pilgrim," we will look at a number of ways to understand home. One way is to understand it as the place you belong. An old meaning of the word *belong* is "nearby, at hand." What is nearby is accessible; it's what authentically feeds the soul. But coming to know where you belong often calls for developing a sensibility that tells you where you do not belong, and we will also explore that sensibility in this chapter.

There will be numerous seductions that may call you to illusions of belonging: fame, popularity, affluence, adoration, and success. You will inevitably take up residency in one or more of these seductions, resulting in *spiritual homelessness*. This is simply the dark path of seeking, calling for enough humility to ask for help. Seeking is, to a great measure, possessing enough mindfulness and resolve to admit you have lost your way. We will explore this critical topic in Chapter 2.

Seekers are asked to remain students of presence. *Presence* is a way to connect with ourselves and others, and in Chapter 3, we will explore how, as a seeker, you are asked to remain intimate with life—renewing your depth of connection with your lived experience. We will look at what it means to live with both a contracted and an expanded presence. Such contrasting presences open us to several important curiosities: What is here now? What is not here now? What is needed? Is this situation asking for more or less of me?

Seekers are midwives, helping some vision of home to be born from the way we hold our injuries, sorrows, joys, and passions. As we refuse to live at a distance from ourselves, our imagination emerges. This refusal demands to know where we belong. And at the threshold, we hold the curiosity that eagerly seeks home, where we now can imagine what might be calling to our true natures. Thus, imagination is the topic of Chapter 4, in which we will explore how culture and family shape imagination, the four energies of imagination (curiosity, novelty, wonder, and creativity), and why the *sacred ordinary* is critical to the seeker developing greater imagination on the way home.

Home means also learning to welcome the unease and restlessness announcing a time for movement. In Chapter 5, "Following Hermes Home," we will examine the benefits of remaining Hermetic, where home takes on the meaning of making peace with movement. As you protest endings less, a new faith accompanies what comes to conclusion. You believe that a birth is unfolding following this passing. You deepen yourself as a seeker when you grieve what was, becoming grateful for what was offered to you and eager to receive what is yet to come.

The energy of longing inspires the seeker—the longing to experience the enchantment of being moved and touched by life. But too often, the enchantment of seeking is replaced by an attachment to protecting ourselves and surviving. In Chapter 6, "Seeking Enchantment," we will look at how we get stuck in disenchantment, with our psyche moving automatically into postures of fighting, fleeing, or freezing. Enchantment depends upon our ability to pause, ground, and calm ourselves. In this chapter we will learn how to feel fear and simultaneously feel safe, setting the stage for an enchanted life.

Seekers are meant to be elders as the result of risking many threshold crossings, and in Chapter 7, "The Aging Seeker," we will explore the difference between *olders* and *elders*. You come to know wisdom as the capacity to hold the entirety of your humanity and the grace needed to welcome the humanity of others. Grace replaces a rigidity of belief, attitude, and spirit with suppleness capable of offering an invitation to those holding a different vision. Death takes nothing from you. You live the old dream to the end. You know your purpose is to devotedly remain a student of life's impenetrable mystery, and in that devotion, to offer other seekers a place to linger during a dark night.

An Invitation

My hope is that you experience this book as a large invitation to sustain the faith that seeking was always what you were meant to do. In the following pages you will discover that as a seeker, you are simply called to live with more courage than is needed by the non-seeker. You have come to know the tension sitting at "the edge"; you know what it means to wrestle at the precipice where the comfort of the familiar meets the agitation calling you to somewhere you have never been.

Ultimately, it can be said of the seeker: time and time again you find yourself embraced by change, now understanding it as simply the heartbeat of life. And as you rest your head upon the chest of life, you now know what you've been seeking. You were always meant to have a deep, intimate relationship with life. What began as two strangers morphed into an abiding kinship and then dropped into an intense love affair. Your life has become a story filled with meaning and opportunity to wonder, allowing yourself to be touched and moved and grateful to have made some small contribution to the flow of life's immensity. You have come home to life and to yourself.

May these pages support, guide, and renew your spirit as a seeker.

> May all that is unforgiven in you
> Be released.
>
> May your fears yield
> Their deepest tranquilities.
>
> May all that is unlived in you
> Blossom into a future
> Graced with Love.
> (John O'Donohue, "To Come Home to Yourself")

1

The Pilgrim

What each must seek in his life never was on land or sea. It is something out of his own unique potentiality for experience, something that never has been and never could have been experienced by anyone else.

—Joseph Campbell

SOME TIME AGO, I WAS engaged in conversation with a colleague regarding the men's groups I facilitate. He asked about the length of time that a man might remain in a group, and I told him the average stay was about seven years. He quickly pointed out that if that was the average stay, then some men stayed as long as eleven years, to which I nodded affirmatively.

"Why would they continue in the group that long?" he asked, more with a tone of condemnation than curiosity.

"They're *seekers*—pilgrims, if you will," I replied.

My colleague's eyes held a downward gaze, his breathing became shallow, and he nodded slightly, which segued us into a different topic. I assumed the topic of men being seekers was not one he wanted to pursue with me.

Our exchange got me thinking that my colleague's reaction was not particularly unusual. It might just be that non-seeking is a much more popular endeavor. And so, before exploring the nature of a seeker, it might be helpful to look at the non-seeker who dwells in each of us.

Non-Seeking

One definition of the word *seeking* is "to look for." Hence, we can say that *non-seeking* means "not looking for." So what are we actually doing when we are not looking for? There are several characteristics of non-seeking, or not looking for.

The first feature of non-seeking is typically being embraced by lethargy. An old meaning of the word *lethargy* is "to become inactive through forgetfulness." What is it that we are actually forgetting when in the grips of lethargy? We are likely forgetting we are pilgrims on a spiritual journey. We begin instead to define ourselves as homesteaders, and we settle into what is currently believed and valued. The homesteader looks away from the vastness and immensity of life in favor of living in a contracted story. From this narrative, old meanings are held onto tightly, resisting life's call to change.

The second quality indicative of non-seeking is a kind of sleep induced by prolonged lethargy. Such a slumber anesthetizes the energies of curiosity, wonder, and longing. As these strengths of spirit are subdued the non-seeker slips into mediocrity, accompanied by melancholy. Non-seekers experience an increased numbing as it becomes more and more difficult to maintain a sensibility to the interior world of instinct, emotion, imagination, and desire.

The third property of non-seeking is a moratorium on a life of self-examination. Non-seekers pretend there is nothing more to know about themselves. No more welcome is offered to their soul's desiring invitation. They no longer hear the pleas of the soul to learn about giving and receiving love, to deepen a capacity for living authentically, to ignite their passion to create, to strengthen their longing for freedom or personal empowerment, or to experience genuine belonging. The restlessness of these denied parts often makes them come to us in the night, banging at the psychic door we've closed on them.

There is a seeker and non-seeker in each of us, and both are energized by tension. The seeker is inspired by the tension created by non-seeking, while the non-seeker is motivated by the tension of seeking. The seeker makes peace with a restlessness that calls him or her to the pilgrimage. The non-seeker is called to pause, maybe for a short while or maybe for an extended period. Two common justifications of such an extended pause include "My whole story has been told; there's nothing else to discover" and "I'm waiting for absolute confirmation that a particular risk is the one to take."

When we slip into the grip of non-seeking, often it's because we have been disillusioned. Some dream has suffered a heavy blow. When a dream dies, it is only too easy to view life and/or God as a cruel parent, not invested in supporting our desires and needs.

Sometimes it is very difficult to find the entitlement either to dream or to dare to manifest a dream. My father was a brilliant self-educated historian who held a vision of formally studying and teaching history. He held a special fondness for the possibility of visiting his favorite historical sites, such as Gettysburg in the United States and Delphi in Greece. He possessed one of the central characteristics of a seeker: he knew what he loved. However, for many reasons, he could not find the entitlement to live his love. He became a victim of his own dream, which taunted him and left him in the grips of a wanting courage. He refused to discover in himself what Campbell would have called his "unique potentiality for experience, something that never could have been experienced by anyone else."

My father's story, like that of other non-seekers, has a tragic element to it: the unlived dream. Yet I am grateful to have been fathered by a man who knew how to dream, teaching me to hold a large vision. Seekers are not simply asked to respond to a desire but to look for what brought more life to those who came before us and will bring more life to those who will come after us. So it's appropriate and fitting for a man to pass to the next generation something asking for fulfillment. My father's legacy was asking me to find enough internal and external support to live what I love. I do this for me, for my father, for his father, and for my son and his son.

I often feel the seduction to take up residency in the land of unlived dreams, where there is no defeat, no risk—and no victory. However, the ultimate defeat may be the refusal to bring the dream to life and risk how challenging life's response might be. With adequate support and the help of the gods, I pray that I might be able to live over and over again the question, what does this legacy ask of me? Typically, the response I hear is a direction calling for some degree of boldness.

This happened with Harold, a forty-five-year-old business executive. Harold came to see me complaining of the stress he was experiencing with his three adult children and, as we soon discovered, in all his relationships. I began to understand his relational challenges as he related to me competitively and with condescension, glibly mocking any suggestion I made. As we talked, it became increasingly clear that Harold had sacrificed the pilgrimage of his maturation in favor of reducing life to a series of businesses. His waking hours were characterized by endless combative exchanges, and he was always striving to have his contentious maneuvers gain him some upper hand.

"Harold, I notice that when I offer you some suggestion that I believe might be helpful, you don't seem to pause in consideration of what you've heard," I pointed out.

"What do I do instead?" he asked, suggesting that he was not cognizant of his reactions to me.

"Well, most of the time you give me several reasons why my recommendation borders on the ridiculous," I explained.

"That's funny, that's what my wife says," he responded, with a smile that appeared forced—attempting to conceal the thought that there might be another way to relate other than the one he had been employing.

It took Harold some time to let go of being incredulous each time I suggested I wanted to be treated with more consideration. It also became increasingly obvious that many folks had written Harold off as a lost cause and that his wife was approaching that same position. Maybe because he began to understand that not only did I expect him to treat me well but that I was also inviting him to treat himself well, he began to soften—leaving his well-groomed bravado outside my office.

The following quote, commonly attributed to the German writer Goethe, says: "Whatever you can do, or dream you can, begin it. Boldness has genius, power, and magic in it." I suggested it might serve Harold to replace his bravado with a genuine boldness. We spoke of bravado as an attempt to conceal feelings of vulnerability and doubt; while boldness, on the other hand, is driven by tenacity and resolve, possessing no attachment to hiding. Boldness carries no covert agenda. I have witnessed both men and women acting boldly, with neither fanfare nor solicitation of admiration. They move with a quiet focus and a burning passion that resemble a betrothal to life. That might be the magic to which Goethe refers.

Seekers

> *In each of us there dwells a pilgrim. It is the part of us*
> *that longs to have direct contact with the sacred.*
> —Phil Cousineau, *The Art of Pilgrimage*

An ancient meaning for the word *pilgrim* is "foreigner." The seeker, or pilgrim, is willing to be a foreigner. We can think of a foreigner as a stranger. Seekers are strangers to a new place, a new idea, and a new way to see life or themselves.

Cousineau suggests that the pilgrim longs to have direct contact with the sacred. There are several old meanings of the word *sacred*. One is "to confirm or ordain what truly matters." When we are in contact with the sacred, we know why we are alive and what deserves our attention. Several years ago while I was leading a weekend retreat, a woman decided to reveal that she was a lesbian, a secret she had been keeping for forty years. As I watched her weep and take in the love and support of the group, I knew I was in the presence of the sacred, the sacredness of her healing.

A second meaning of the word *sacred* is "to sacrifice." As a foreigner, the seeker sacrifices the familiar. What do we actually sacrifice when we step away from the familiar? We let go of a comfort and an ease offered by well-worn attitudes capable of messaging self-doubt. Beliefs that once brought a great deal of comfort are now up for review.

Marcel Proust suggests that "the voyage of discovery is not in seeking new landscapes but in having new eyes." What experiences have you had that changed the way you see the world? What experiences have helped change how you see yourself? The curiosity of seekers has the power of transforming their eyes as they are touched and moved toward new and different considerations. The eyes of the seeker can be powerfully impacted by openings of the heart.

The poet Rainer Maria Rilke suggests this idea of becoming larger because of love, saying "Love is at first not anything that means merging, giving over, and uniting with another . . . it is a high inducement to the individual to ripen, to become something in himself, to become world, to become world for himself for another's sake." One way we can understand this "ripening" is as an expansion of our ability to see.

The seeker understands the lyric from an old rock tune, "Life is much more than we are," and wants to be touched by that "more." Seekers are willing to encounter what is strange and different, stepping away from the familiar, being at times strangers to themselves and to life, questing new vision.

Questing Vision

Seekers are looking for new vision and will inevitably find themselves going in and out of being in the midst of a *vision quest*. Traditionally, the vision quest was a time of passage where the initiate was to gain more clarity pertaining to his or her life's purpose. How convenient it would be to receive an epiphany defining the essence of our lives. However, given our evolving natures, we're lucky to get a single piece of understanding regarding why we came to the planet.

The quest can be seen as comprising three stages. The first stage is *separation* from familiar people, places, or simply our accustomed way at looking at life. This stage is marked by a desire for something not currently available. It is about the willingness to be a foreigner. It also means being willing to have a relationship with the unknown, guided by curiosity and acceptance. The quester must lean into the journey, not constantly protesting that which is not appealing.

Audrey Hepburn reminded us of this kind of acceptance when she said, "I decided, very early on, just to accept life unconditionally; I never expected it to do anything special for me, yet I seemed to accomplish far more than I had ever hoped. Most of the time it just happened to me without my ever seeking it." She reminded us that although the quest begins with a desire to look for something, it serves us to hold our desire with a gentle grip, allowing life to prod, push, touch, and move us. Questions of the separation stage include: What do I want? What or whom must I leave? Where am I going? Who's coming with me?

The second stage of the quest is a series of tests, sometimes referred to as the *ordeal*. These tests are mostly meant to awaken us. Our attention and sensibilities are heightened as we feel challenged, lost, and bewildered. Questions accompanying the ordeal include: What internal and external resources do I possess that will help me discover what I'm looking for? What is life presenting to me and how does it make me feel? What else do I need to consider? Am I accessing the help available to me? Does the situation I'm in call for me to exercise more will or more acceptance?

The third stage is the *return,* when we integrate what we have learned. In some way, we are already in possession of what we were looking for. As Thomas Merton said, "We have what we seek. . . . It is there all the time, and if we give it time, it will make itself known to us." At this point the tests subside and we turn to how to live with what we have acquired. Questions supporting the return stage include: How can I best bring my new vision into my life? What else can I learn from the vision I've acquired? What service can this new vision bring to my life and to the people of my life? What support will I need in order to integrate what I'm learning? What new level of self-care has been introduced to me?

One indication that we are in the midst of a vision quest is that it becomes fairly obvious that more is happening to us than the original plan of looking for something. It begins to feel as if something is looking for us, or as the Sufi Rumi suggested, "What you seek is seeking you."

Such an experience recently happened for me while attending a symposium in Galway, Ireland. I had gone looking for more information about the impact the god Hermes has on a healing relationship. During the middle of the week, Rob, the organizer of the symposium (who meticulously attended to our needs), suggested we attend a show featuring traditional Irish music and dance. With Rob's encouragement, my wife Connie and I decided to attend the next performance. Upon our arrival, we were pleasantly surprised to see we were part of only several hundred people, scattered in a semicircle and stretching back only seven or eight rows from the stage. Each seat offered great proximity to the performers.

The producer of the show played the guitar and introduced each act, shifting from Irish folk dancing to vocals and then to instrumentals. Shortly into the evening, he introduced a musician who played the Irish pipes, describing in detail the difficulty facing anyone interested in mastering this instrument. I had never heard the Irish pipes and gave the music my full attention.

Within a matter of seconds, I began to sob uncontrollably. I bawled nonstop for about thirty minutes, with an occasional respite to reassure Connie that I was OK and not going to tumble into a heap. I went in and out of feeling embarrassed as the rest of the audience applauded with exuberance and I wept. My tears began to announce an odd weaving of grief and joy, as some unknown part of me felt deeply called by the pipes.

As we rode back on the shuttle to the hotel, I felt gratitude for the opportunity to have witnessed such talent. The dancers moved with passion and grace, while the musicians played their instruments and the vocalists sang lyrics that possessed a soulful resonance. There was a mysterious tone and quality to the movements and sounds, suggesting an offering being made that far transcended the three hundred present in the audience; it felt as if it were all being performed for multiple generations, those past and those yet to come. For my part, I only knew that the pipes had called to me and that my body had recognized the call. And for now, I was willing simply to hold the mystery of the pipes' call.

Within twenty-four hours of the show, I began to learn that the Irish do not refer to a potato famine in their history; they refer to what happened in Ireland from 1845 to 1852 as the Great Hunger. Only the potato was impacted by the blight. All other crops flourished. However, the British owned the land and made it unlawful for the Irish to eat other crops, making the starvation of a people inevitable. Many were so malnourished that they would die aboard ship, unable to complete the fourteen-day crossing to North America.

I decided the pipes were calling me to understand what my great-great-grandfather Michael Ryan had faced during the Great Hunger. I also decided I needed to go to the village of Ardagh, where he lived as a boy.

Upon arriving in Ardagh, I was struck by how small the village was and how old the buildings were—the only facelift belonging to the Catholic church in town. I went to the parish house to investigate the records kept by the church and was greeted sternly by a priest my own age, who questioned the purpose of my visit. When I explained I was seeking some information about my great-great-grandfather, he let me into a musty-smelling dining room with record books scattered all over the table. The books were laid on the table with the air of being in constant use, like the morning newspaper. I had completed some research when the priest pointed out that the parish had suffered a fire in 1841 and that birth records related to a Michael Ryan had likely been destroyed.

I left Ardagh not deeply disappointed but thankful that I had come and sat a bit in the village of Michael Ryan. I also remained curious as to whether the pipes were calling me to something else, something I had yet to identify.

Our last two days were to be spent in Dublin. At any one time during the day, several hundred folks can be seen crossing the bridges that traverse the River Liffey, which runs through the middle of Dublin. At one point, we left a coffee shop and made our way across one of the bridges. As soon as I stepped off the bridge, I noticed my wallet was gone—with about $400 and lots of identification.

The clerk at our hotel advised me to go to the police department and file a report of the theft. As I stood in line at the police department, my energies shifted from shame for acting so negligently, having put my wallet in my back pocket, to gratitude that I had left my passport at the hotel, which would allow me to fly home.

Initially, I wanted to characterize this incident on the River Liffey as just completely unfortunate, bad, regretful, and stupid on my part. This was not what I had been looking for—or was it? I had wanted to know my great-great-grandfather's experience, and so I did. It would have been on this river, making his way to the coast in order to board a ship for America, that he'd probably felt violated, accompanied by a loss of his identity. It was exactly how I felt.

I arrived home in the United States twenty-four hours later and was greeted by an e-mail from a man in Dublin, communicating that he had found my wallet at a bike station and would forward it to me. The wallet arrived twenty-one days later, containing no cash but with all forms of identification intact.

I continue to live in this vision quest, with more understanding of the trauma that befell my ancestors and the legacy that comes to me. I also wonder about the identity I may have forgotten or lost along the way and what identity may be seeking me. Such is the way of the vision quest, keeping me close to some threshold the pipes continue to call to me too.

Threshold Dwellers

Seekers are *threshold dwellers*. They live at the place where "what is" and "what might be" greet one another. They straddle two worlds. They are sensitive to a loss of deeper meaning. Instead of taking sanctuary in life as it is, they are disturbed and agitated, longing for something more relevant that feeds their souls. Seekers want to see what lies beyond. As Joy Page said, "After an eternity of seeking, the sudden threshold of seeing and finding leaves one filled with a strange paradox of ecstasy and grief. I was born to see." Could it be that we were all born ready to stand at the doorway of what might be and allow ourselves to see?

I appreciate the thinking that we were all born to see but that early on in our lives we receive verbal and nonverbal edicts not to see. To illustrate this, I will share with you my experience with William, a forty-two-year-old high school teacher who came to see me with the presenting problem of his wife's drinking.

"I just can't imagine how I've managed to be with a woman for fifteen years and not see how she abuses alcohol!" explained William, chastising himself for his delayed awareness.

"I hear it is difficult for you to accept the timing of your awareness," I replied.

"Very difficult. I can't imagine how I got myself to be looking the other way for such a long time," he lamented.

"I wonder if there was some kind of encouragement in your family of origin not to see what might have been difficult for your family to deal with," I prompted.

William shook his head, perplexed about where he might have learned to look away from what was painful. But a week later he returned, eager to recount the story of Christmas Eve when he was eleven.

"All week I was flooded with memories of a Christmas Eve when I was a kid," he shared, leaning forward, anticipating the opportunity to tell his story. "I was eleven at the time, and it was about five o'clock on Christmas Eve. My four-year-old brother and I always looked forward to going to the family gathering at our grandmother's on Christmas Eve.

"My father came home and went directly upstairs to bed. Our mother followed our father upstairs carrying her vacuum cleaner, more like a weapon than a custodial tool. She had hardly reached the top of the stairs when we heard that vacuum cleaner roaring. But within moments, the sound of the vacuum cleaner stopped, replaced by our father's yelling, 'Get that damn thing out of here!' We then witnessed the vacuum cleaner smashing into the bottom of the stairs.

"It was obvious that the vacuum had not slipped out of our mother's hand but had been tossed down the stairs by our father. The incident scared my brother and me. As our mother retrieved her vacuum cleaner and prepared to place it back in the closet, she looked over at us and said, 'Your father has the flu.'

"By the time I became a teenager, I figured out that my father was drunk that Christmas Eve and had aggressively thrown the vacuum cleaner down the stairs. My mother had invited me not to see what was really happening. The combination of feeling scared and wanting to remain loyal to her skewed my vision, not allowing me to see what actually was happening. I later realized that that Christmas Eve demonstrated my father's alcoholism, which would impact my entire life."

William allowed himself some moments of silence so his body could catch up with what he had remembered. He then turned to me with a knowing in his eyes, and he explained how his fear and loyalty had also prevented him from seeing the severity of his wife's drinking.

The questions holding the potential emancipation of our ability to see include the following: How was I told not to see? What was I told not to see? Is there some loyalty asking to be betrayed? If I see, what do I lose? So, to stand at the threshold with wide-open eyes, we may need to visit some old fear, pain, or loyalty that had us closing our eyes. This self-examination at the threshold will call for the courage to address the seductions that happen there.

Threshold Seductions

Four *seductions* normally occur at a threshold, diminishing our capacity to seek and therefore our ability to make a threshold crossing. These seductions are meant to help us remain risk avoidant:

1. **"Life is too big."** This seduction suggests that we will simply be overwhelmed by life if we dare flirt with a threshold crossing. This thinking is typically accompanied by imaging catastrophic events that will occur on the other side of the threshold.

2. **"I'm too small."** This seduction is the first cousin of "Life is too big." The tendency here is to diminish ourselves, as incapable, and simply not in possession of enough intelligence or astuteness to deal with life's challenges. With this seduction there is often an attachment to feeling either greatly ambivalent or confused about ways to circumvent a threshold crossing.

3. **"Life is small."** Nothing insults life more than this seduction. The delusion accompanying this seduction is, "If I define life as small, nothing big and unmanageable will happen to me." Life responds with tests and demands, refusing to be placed in our small bio-boxes.

4. **"I'm too big."** Of course, this is the first cousin of "Life is small." There is an arrogance here suggesting we are bigger than life. Again, as we are presented with catastrophic illness, the loss of loved ones, or the loss of employment, we are invited to loosen our grip on pride and get honest about our fear.

Typically, a number of questions must be faced at the threshold, such as these:

- Am I presently at a threshold?
- Will I see things at the threshold that will be painful?
- Will it be difficult to accept choices I've made on the way to the threshold?
- Will I be separating from someone I love if I cross the threshold?
- Will I receive the help I need to understand what awaits me at the threshold?
- Will I be asked to let go of time-tested beliefs at the threshold?
- Will I get lost as I step through the threshold?
- How am I likely to prevent myself from making a threshold crossing?

Threshold Crossings

We recently acquired a seven-month-old Nordic Golden Retriever. As he approached the threshold of the nursery where he had been housed all his life, he dropped to the ground, protesting his advance. My initial response was to say, "Oh, come on—what's the big deal!" Then I paused and reminded myself that his world was about to become exponentially larger. Connie and I began offering verbal and nonverbal gestures of reassurance. Finally, the breeder intervened, giving Bo a forceful tug into his new world.

I began to wonder if we all might need gentle reassurance at the threshold, as well as an occasional push into unknown worlds. In any case, some form of support and guidance seems absolutely necessary during a threshold crossing. Our courage during a threshold crossing reflects some part of us that dies while something else is being birthed. Although life is essentially about change, the ego indulges in the belief that it can eclipse life's continuous endings and beginnings. However, as pilgrims we are asked to accept the responsibility of recreating ourselves again and again. It may be this act of recreating ourselves that reflects the sacredness of our essential natures.

Recreating Ourselves

> *To dare is to lose one's footing momentarily. Not to dare is to lose oneself.*
>
> —Soren Kierkegaard

Our culture's obsession with heroes and magnificent deeds suggests that daring is more of an exhibit of bravado than a case of losing one's footing. However, Kierkegaard's assertion reminds us of who we are. We are not finished products. Our daring is not about some flamboyant display of an unusual talent. The daring that occurs during a threshold crossing is about recreating ourselves.

As Rollo May said, "Clearly self-creating is actualized by our hopes, our ideals, our images, and all sorts of imagined constructs that we may hold from time to time in the forefront of our attention." The ego takes satisfaction in believing that its current hopes, ideals, and images constitute a finished identity, not one that is in need of some new birth.

We can understand a threshold crossing as a birthing process. We may be acquiring a new belief, a new value, a new intention, or an even greater permission to feel. But as noted above, all births entail some ending. Something is dying as something is beginning. Threshold crossings call for the courage to die. And as cancer survivor Mark Nepo says, "All courage is a threshold crossing."

The death of some expression of magical thinking often occurs at a threshold crossing. We employ magic in childhood to comfort ourselves and create an alleged feeling of security. Some of these magical beliefs include: "If I work hard enough, I will be seen and appreciated," "If I am kind to others, they will be kind to me," "If I love enough, I can overcome any problem that comes up between me and others," "If I give enough, I will get my needs met," "Good things will happen if I am adaptive and not disruptive," and "If I bring the right people into my life, I won't be hurt."

Of course, fate will be fraught with enough danger and hazards to shake and in some cases tear magic from our psychic grasp. This is likely one reason Nietzsche suggested that we should embrace *Amor fati*, or love of fate. An ancient meaning of the word *fate* is "ordained by the gods." Fate has the tendency of calling us out of childhood into deeper levels of maturation and a more sustainable relationship with life.

There are two dangers we face if we do not have enough support during a threshold crossing. The first is that we may not give ourselves enough permission to grieve the loss of magical thinking employed in childhood and the losses we accrued attempting to live by magical guidance. The second danger is that some level of cynicism can easily slip into our mindset as some magical thinking dies. We may tell ourselves, "I was trying to make life something kind of neat when all along it just sucked." We may need help to understand that just because naïveté dies, that doesn't mean life is awful.

The seductive threshold illusion is that a death only takes place if we make a threshold crossing. A larger death occurs when we do not make a crossing. We are pilgrims! We will be moving in one direction or the other. If we are not up to recreating ourselves, then we will experience a contraction of the self.

Anita, the seventy-two-year-old founder and executive director of a shelter for homeless and unwed mothers, came in for her first appointment. She immediately began to identify the reason for her appointment.

"I have mentored many women through the years," she reported. "I have seen what can happen for women when they are willing to heal and hold a vision of empowering themselves." But she seemed to lack any sense of satisfaction regarding such success.

"I am familiar with your work," I said, "and it is extremely commendable."

"It may be commendable, but I've begun to wonder about my work with myself," she said, explicitly expressing a feeling of disappointment.

"Tell me more about this work with yourself."

"Well, I'm noticing that some of these young women have outgrown me," she explained.

"Do you mean that they no longer need your services?"

"No, I mean they have more growth than I do," she exclaimed, with a tone of disgust.

"How do you know that?"

"I listen to the issues they face, how they take care of themselves, and how they handle adversity," she said.

"I'm hearing that you see something in them that you don't see in yourself."

"I do, and in some cases, they are twenty years younger than me," she offered, her voice deepening.

"Have you been on pause?"

"What do you mean?" she asked, leaning forward.

"You have lived with a commitment to mindful living and have attended to the growth supportive of such a life. So what happened?"

"Maybe I did pause and these young women just went past me," she said.

"Do you understand how you came to decide to pause?"

"No, I don't understand it," she said. "But more than pausing, I see my thinking, attitudes, and self-esteem returning to an earlier time in my life."

Our work soon revealed that Anita's choice to pause reflected her story that if she continued making threshold crossings, she ran the risk of generating some significant distance between her and her husband. She did not trust that her husband would join her. Her threshold-crossing resistance was matching her husband's. She was experiencing some important losses related to self-care and how she was relating to others. Anita began moving toward her next threshold crossing as I suggested she think seriously about offering emotional leadership in her marriage and that she renew her connection to her desire as a way to guide her choices.

Anita became acquainted with the great paradox of the human spirit, whose essence is change. Spirit remains on the move, either moving into creative and constructive forms or destructive and noncreative forms. As a pilgrim, it longs for an experience of the sacred, and if inhibited with enough fear, it settles for movement back toward something more primitive. The notion of pause is a euphemism for the lack of creative movement.

Interrupting Legacies

Nothing haunts a threshold crossing more than the ghost of a debilitating legacy. We can think of a *legacy* as an attitude, belief, feeling, or behavior aimed at offering us some level of protection. The dilemma is that it is only too easy to live in the influence of a legacy, whether we need the protection or not. When the threshold crossing feels weighed down, thick with fear and hopelessness, it is likely the pressure of a haunting legacy calling us back to what has been familiar for generations. It is similar to summoning enough courage to resist strong peer pressure calling us to adopt the vision of the crowd. We may even feel as if we are betraying something or someone by crossing over, without any real understanding of the betrayal. We may be asked at the threshold to interrupt a legacy of voices lacking heart.

> You can't, if you can't feel it, if it never
> Rises from your soul, and sways
> The heart of every single hearer,
> With deepest power, in simple ways.
> You'll sit forever, gluing things together,
> Cooking up a stew from other's scraps,
> Blowing on a miserable fire,
> Made from your heap of dying ash.
> Let apes and children praise your art,
> If their admiration's to your taste,
> But you'll never speak from heart to heart,
> Unless it rises up from your heart's space.
> (Goethe, *Faust: First Part*)

Goethe reminds us that a threshold crossing likely involves something rising up from your heart's space. What rises up is often a longing to let go of whatever blocks our hearts in the name of making us feel safe.

Dangers Facing the Seeker

Four essential dangers readily face seekers. The first danger is the impact the dream has upon those currently attached to non-seeking, as depicted in the following Old Testament quote:

> And when they saw him afar off, even before he came near unto them, they conspired against him to slay him. And they said one to another, Behold, this dreamer cometh. Come now, therefore, and let us slay him, and cast him into some pit, and we will say, Some evil beast hath devoured him: and we shall see what will become of his dreams.
>
> (Gen. 37:18–20)

The fact that seekers often hold visions of greater compassion and peace does not suggest that their dreams are not highly disruptive. We can see this understanding of disruption created by the seeker when Christ said, "Do not suppose that I have come to bring peace to the earth. I did not come to bring peace, but a sword. For I have come to turn a man against his father, a daughter against her mother, a daughter-in-law against her mother-in-law—a man's enemies will be the members his own household." (Matthew 10:34–36) The seeker's vision of what might be is typically at the heart of most radical change. Hence, the dream of the seeker acts like a sword separating vision from status quo and from those who dwell there.

The second danger to the seeker is taking up residency in the vision of what might be rather than knowing how to make peace with what is present and real now. As Herman Hesse said, "What could I say to you that would be of value, except that perhaps you seek too much, that as a result of your seeking you cannot find?" Hesse's wisdom suggests that seeking often calls for the courage to be still, to allow what we seek to touch and move us. Seeking can be a very forward-moving energy, pushing us past what we are looking for. Pausing may be one of the great secrets of seeking.

The great paradox is that as much as it takes courage to make a threshold crossing, it also takes courage to keep one foot in the present. Threshold dwellers can easily be seduced into dwelling in the dream, where they are immune from risks and the perils of ordinary life, or possibly, as with Nietzsche's vision, as a way to escape the arduous task of self-love.

The Swiss psychiatrist Carl Jung understood that Nietzsche fell prey to such a seduction, and Jung did not want it happening to himself: "The root of the whole thing is that Nietzsche is equal to Zarathustra [a Persian prophet], so the two figures are mixed together. Therefore all the trouble, the whole tragedy." Jung was aware that Nietzsche lived in his own vision of Zarathustra, making it nearly impossible for Nietzsche to embody the longings and the love of an ordinary man seeking deeper meaning. This was a tragedy Jung wanted to avoid.

The third danger facing the seeker is the tendency to fall into bad faith and cynicism. The larger the vision, the more variables there are determining its manifestation and the less control the seeker has to make it happen. Seekers can forget that life will always be much larger than them and their vision. As an old mentor of mine often said, "Maturity is about dreaming, becoming deeply disillusioned, and dreaming again."

The fourth danger facing seekers is self-righteousness. It can be very easy for us to look at the crowd satisfying themselves with the status quo and becoming parochial in their vision—and decide we are superior. Self-righteousness often reflects falling prey to forgetting how to authentically love ourselves. There is a tendency to employ a hierarchical lens, seeing ourselves at the top of the heap and others at the bottom.

Care for the Seeker

The first act of self-care for the seeker is to travel with other seekers. If our vision or threshold crossing is experienced as disruptive to the views of others, then those others can easily project a myriad of characteristics onto the seeker. If the disruption is experienced as frightening, then others will likely ascribe negative characteristics to the seeker. If the disruption makes them feel inspired, then they will project extremely positive traits onto the seeker.

I often say that seekers run the risk of being either demonized or deified. In either case, who they actually are can be either missed or ignored. Legend has it that on his deathbed, Confucius was asked by his students and followers if he had a final wish. He uttered, "Don't deify me." Many of his devotees would not honor his request and went ahead and vaulted him to celestial status.

Seekers need to keep close their genuine friends, people offering acceptance as well as readiness to confront. Such relationships are infused with truth telling and compassion. These friends know one another's failures, sufferings, longings, and loves. They know how to cherish the offerings of support they receive. They use their best wisdom to call each other back to themselves when they have fallen under some enchantment or distraction.

The second form of self-care for the seeker is to continue to learn how to remain grounded in what is. As Bodhidarma said, "People of this world are deluded. They're always longing for something—always, in a word, seeking." As in the case of Nietzsche tumbling into his vision of Zarathustra, there is a lure toward living in the dream, where we might take an extended respite from our spiritual task.

No one understood this seduction and its price better than Viktor Frankl, who spent time in a Nazi concentration camp. Of that experience, he said, "We had to learn ourselves and, furthermore, we had to teach the despairing men, that it did not really matter what we expected from life, but rather what life expected of us. . . . Life ultimately means taking the responsibility to find the right answers to its problems and to fulfill the task which it constantly sets for each individual."

The third expression of self-care is to expect to be disillusioned. When the seeker falls into disappointment and discouragement, it is helpful for him to experience the felt presence of friends who are familiar with the challenge. It can also be helpful for him to ask: "What illusion am I being asked to let go of? What loss do I need to grieve? How can I make meaning out of my experience without making it into a catastrophe?" The challenge for the seeker is to resist becoming a victim of fate, thereby reducing life to an enemy. Seekers are asked to express their disappointment, which may be gut-wrenching, and return to being a student of life.

The fourth act of self-care is to address the possibility of falling into self-righteousness. Such a fall happens as we compare ourselves to others and aggrandize our heroic threshold crossings. It is very helpful to remember the deeply personal nature of our crossings. They are meant to deepen our relationship to our own uniqueness. We can also remind ourselves of the deeply personal nature of the other's path, which will inevitably be shrouded in mystery for us.

Self-righteousness is an attempt to prove our personal worth, suggesting we have walked away from valuing ourselves. All the comparing and contrasting we do, with the result being some temporary boost, will not restore a much-needed abiding self-love. We can get serious about the restoration of our self-worth by asking some important questions: Have I given the responsibility of finding me lovable to someone else? Is there something I need to forgive myself for? What is at risk if I choose to love myself? Am I willing to interrupt any attachment I might have to perfectionism?

It will also serve seekers to take the experience of spiritual homelessness seriously. Having enough clarity to identify where we do not belong and to summon enough courage to move away from where we do not belong will help us to navigate our way home. We will explore this further in the next chapter.

A Blessing for the Seeker

The same contractions that pushed and nudged you from the comfort and repose of your mother's womb will again and again announce the presence of some threshold awaiting you. May you be received with welcome whenever you dare to be born again.

That initial incubation was meant to prepare you for something larger. You were, from your conception, destined to be a seeker—pilgrimaging to ever larger worlds. These crossings will sometimes be held up with excitement and anticipation and, at other times, weighed down with the energies of fear and ambivalence.

Life will announce some threshold crossing, as did the tension pulsating on your mother's uterine wall. You will be disturbed by loss, mediocrity, suffering, bewilderment, and betrayal—tensions asking you to look for something you may simply know as larger and nothing else.

These threshold crossings, or births, are why you came to the Earth. You have been asked to author a life—to create a unique expression of the human condition that is you. Similar to the ignorance you possessed about your first breath, your threshold crossings will often find you wanting for some knowing you have yet to possess.

At the threshold, knowing must be replaced by longing, timidity replaced by boldness, and pretense replaced by courage. There will be a tone of your lineage announcing some ancestral deprivation that kept those who came before you in a smaller story. And now you are asked to shed an old loyalty, preparing to feed some old hunger the bread of freedom, compassion, love, and belonging.

You are asked to be neither naive nor cynical about dreaming. Your dream may threaten those who have stopped dreaming. Rather than feel victimized by their fear, walk with your brother and sister who call you back to yourself when you lose your way, seduced by some enchantment or distraction.

You are a seeker—the one asked to step toward the sacred transcendent that lies beyond this moment and toward the sacred ordinary sitting before you in this present time. You are asked to surrender to a deep restlessness and a quiet presence.

May these births, these pilgrimages, teach you when to move, when to be still, when to ask for help, and when to be grateful. And then the tone of your life will be in rhythm with the opus the gods have ordained for you.

2

Spiritual Homelessness

If you are homeless or about to be homeless, call -------.
—Sign on the wall at Bridewell Police Station,
Chancey Street, Dublin, Ireland

As I STOOD IN LINE preparing to give a police report about my lost wallet, I was mesmerized by the statement above regarding homelessness. I was aware that the posted announcement referred to anyone lacking concrete shelter. However, I felt the presence of a larger declaration, one I could not immediately decipher. I was still in shock, having hours before been pickpocketed on the O'Connell Bridge. Before leaving the police station, I felt compelled to look back at the sign one more time. What was this sign asking of me?

More clarity began to break through as the fog of shock lifted. I felt homeless and I wanted to go home. At least for me, there was something on the other side of the ocean I called home—unlike my great-great-grandfather Michael Ryan, whose oceanic crossing promised very little.

When I finally arrived home to the town and house where I reside, I experienced a palpable sense of comfort. I began easing myself into larger curiosities about home, wondering if perhaps there is a greater consideration about home that goes beyond that of a roof over our heads. Does anything beyond a familiar environment constitute home? What truly is home? And are many of us experiencing a kind of spiritual homelessness?

Let's look at what home means to the seeker and what to do when we find ourselves spiritually homeless.

Sharpening the View of Home

Seekers are asked to sharpen their view of home. Odysseus longed to reach his home of Ithaca, even while being asked to experience the journey itself as home. It's the same with all seekers: they are asked to be clear about what they truly seek and to open to experiencing the journey as home.

Some old meanings of the word *home* include "where we choose to linger," and "familiar and personal." We can begin to hold a larger vision of home when asking these questions: What calls me to linger? Where do I create familiarity? Who knows me? Do I maintain a devotion to know myself? Who do I want to know?

Most important for seekers is to hold some deep awareness of homelessness, indicating where they do *not* belong. By *spiritual homelessness*, I am suggesting an experience of soul. The soul lingers where it is fed, and it feeds on at least four distinct levels: boundaries providing protection and safety, encouragement, nurturance, and discipline. We can think of these four ingredients as the parenting offerings we initially needed as children and will continue to need, whether they come from ourselves or from others. Let's look closer at each of these.

Boundaries Providing Protection and Safety

The soul feeds on boundaries providing protection and safety: we tend to linger where we feel safe. A homeless soul typically feels unsafe due to inadequate boundaries that would protect against physical or emotional harm. It is worth noting that folks who were raised in a home where brutality was a daily routine often do not feel safe where there are good boundaries, since the notion of effective boundaries is foreign. They are often spiritual orphans, finding more safety in the nomadic life. They knew the utter vulnerability of being in one place with the same people, and they learned early to remain a moving target. They learned that it is the people closest that are the most dangerous, so remaining detached and at a distance feels safer. Emotional proximity equals danger. Their strength is in their autonomy and self-reliance.

Whether we come from a highly traumatic background or from a family that simply had its share of dysfunction, we remain spiritually homeless when as adults, we employ childhood strategies aimed at supporting safety. Unless there is reason to have some important awakening, most of us will continue to employ tactics that have long lost their usefulness for purposes of safety. *Merger* is an example of a childhood strategy aimed at generating safety. The child does psychologically what boxers do with their bodies when they are fatigued. They hug one another, making it difficult for the opponent to launch a crushing blow. Psychological merger sends the following messages: "I'll do my best to cooperate," "I won't get in the way," and "I'm only here to be helpful."

My client Marie was an example of someone who used this strategy. A forty-five-year-old ER nurse, she came to see me complaining about feeling used by everyone.

"I feel used by my minister, friends, colleagues, and family members," she expressed, with a note of exhaustion and confusion.

"Sounds like your life is not your own and you don't know how that happened," I added.

"No! I have no idea what it means to have my own life!" she exclaimed, her confusion morphing into anger.

"I'd like to hear how you lost your life."

Because of ineffective boundaries, Marie was feeling spiritually homeless. She spent a number of sessions detailing the brutality her father had enacted upon her and her two brothers. She had spent her childhood either desperately attempting to stay out of reach of her father's ruthless attacks or sending him a message of complete compliance—the latter being her efforts to merge.

"I can't imagine you ever dared say no to your father or challenge his authority," I suggested.

"I did what I was told, but it wasn't ever enough to stop the abuse," she explained, her gaze dropping under the weight of years of helplessness.

I then began to notice an energy, mostly emanating from her eyes, resembling a tractor beam. My immediate inclination was to think she was extending an invitation to deepen our rapport. However, over time it became apparent that she extended a similar invitation to everyone, with no discrimination. It was difficult for her to admit that her childhood exercise of merger had translated into adult seduction. But her flirtations had no sexual agenda; they were all about attempting to create safety.

Marie discovered that her soulful homelessness was to a great degree about her inability to say no. She knew that any form of separation from her father's expectations would have been dangerous, and that saying no now would to some degree separate her from others. She slowly learned that honoring her unique needs and wishes did separate her from others, but not in some dangerous way. She began to report feeling more relaxed around people as she worked less at feverishly calling people to her. Slowly, she acquired a new vitality as she shifted from attempts at merger to being authentic.

Marie's progress mirrored what Alice Miller described when she said, "Where there had been only fearful emptiness or equally frightening grandiose fantasies, an unexpected wealth of vitality is now discovered. This is not a homecoming, since this home has never before existed. It is the creation of home." Marie was learning that she could be separate from others and that it would not lead to complete isolation and death. She was creating a home based upon the employment of boundaries that supported her safety and the uniqueness of her needs and beliefs. She was learning that this home could be shared with others, as long as there was mutual respect for one another's worldview.

Encouragement

We linger where we feel encouraged. An old meaning of the word *encourage* is "to inspire with courage." We feel encouraged when we experience an infusion of a life force supporting us to live from our hearts, from our core. When there is no heartening to know and live our passion, we are spiritually homeless, with no call to linger.

A number of years ago I expressed to my mentor, George, how grateful I felt for his encouragement. He asked what I was most thankful for pertaining to his encouragement. I responded, "When I walk away from me, you call me back to myself." We sat in silence, appreciating the sweetness of lingering in each other's company.

Stepping away from spiritual homelessness may mean getting clear about where you receive encouragement. Who knows you and wants to know you? Who applauds the expression of your uniqueness? Who offers a heartening of your sorrow and your joy? Who celebrates your gifts? Who encourages your passion?

Nurturing

We also linger where we feel nurtured. Feeling nurtured is about feeling cared for. We linger where our well-being is prioritized. Our well-being is valued where there is comfort and ease. However, to move into more ease we sometimes need to become more resilient to hearing the truth from those who know us well. This is especially true when their input is about something we've been denying, like drinking to excess, being irresponsible with money, or not managing our anger.

I often ask folks, "How do you get nurtured?" The question is commonly met with confusion, suggesting that nurturance is a somewhat foreign concept to them. Here are some suggestions regarding sources of nurturance: friends who hear and understand you, hot baths, nutritious food, naps, getting held, therapeutic massage, restorative yoga, listening to music, playing, and experiencing beauty. As John O'Donohue said, "The Beautiful offers us an invitation to order, coherence, and unity. When these needs are met, the soul feels at home in the world." In addition, when gratitude accompanies our experience of beauty, we feel gifted and cared for. Suddenly, the majesty of a sunset becomes an offering of the gods, and we are touched to be the recipients of such rapture.

Discipline

Lastly, we linger because of a sense of discipline. The common contemporary understanding of the word *discipline* suggests focus, personal determination, and willpower. An old meaning of the word comes from the word *discipleship*. From this viewpoint, collaboration and co-creation are perspectives aimed at approaching concrete or psychological tasks. In either case, we linger because there are resources, there is help, and we are not alone.

When we live the meaning of discipline as staunchness, we run the risk of isolation and feeling overwhelmed. The more isolated and overwhelmed we are, the more likely it is that we will fall into burnout. Depleted energy skews our vision of where and with whom we should linger, resulting in spiritual homelessness.

Belonging to Ourselves

The paradox for us seekers is that we are called to be at home and to pursue a larger vision of home. Our lives must be somewhat nomadic in order that we may pursue a larger vision.

The nomadic life can make a very significant offering regarding ownership. What does it mean to own something? It seems to suggest we have control over something. If we own land, we can live on it, sell it, rent it, or give it away. Often the illusion of permanence accompanies ownership. Another seduction of ownership is that it tends to pull us away from our interior worlds as the place we call home. We identify people, places, and things as home, all of which we have diminished control over. There is much more control in the interior life, where we can give ourselves permission to feel, intuit, imagine, and love. We can also bring credibility to these internal states, crafting them at the core of our character. The gift of the nomadic is the reminder of non-permanence in the outer world, referring us back to our inner worlds.

There must be a place to linger, even for a while, where we remember who we are and feel touched by the warm gaze of a welcome. In the pause we call home, we know we are not alone. Our pursuits and our separateness receive a temporary respite as we feel held by friends, maybe by a stranger, and maybe even by the gods. Seekers are asked to learn to hold the tension of deep renewal and a restlessness spirited by wonder.

We do not find the sacred by parading about and giving testimony to some beloved dogma. The sacred responds favorably to our heartful longing to be in its presence. We are asked to become familiar with the sanctity of our longing to be deeply connected to ourselves. When our longing to belong to ourselves is thwarted or inhibited, we fall into spiritual homelessness.

Self-Alienation

> *Man's feeling of homelessness, of alienation, has been intensified in the midst of a bureaucratized, impersonal mass society. He has come to feel himself an outsider even within his own human society. He is trebly alienated: a stranger to God, to nature, and to the gigantic social apparatus that supplies his material wants. But the worst and final form of alienation, toward which indeed the others tend, is a man's alienation from his own self.*
> —William Barrett

There are four ways in which we become susceptible to self-alienation: being externally referenced, becoming a victim, oversizing or undersizing ourselves, and excessively protecting our hearts. Let's examine each of these in more detail.

External Referencing

Barrett reminds us that the worst form of alienation is alienation from the self. When we are estranged from ourselves, we no longer belong to ourselves. We have lost a devotion to be familiar with ourselves. We have lost home.

What pulls us away from ourselves, or how do we end up creating such a great distance from ourselves? We do it once we are taught to be externally referenced. This happens naturally as we are socialized. We learn what our parents and families expect of us. We seek their love and approval, and so we become skilled at reading their expectations and delivering appropriately. Our external reference to our families flows easily to teachers, clergy, coaches, and peers. We refer to the expectations that sit outside of us, beginning to ignore our interior bodily and emotional reactions to life. Safety, love, and success take on meanings belonging to others. We do not belong with others—we belong to them. Our personal meanings of love and success fade into the distance.

The homelessness created by being externally referenced leaves us fundamentally powerless to create and define ourselves; we wait for others to tell us who we are. However, several severe challenges accompany our pause. First, we may not be given enough information to tell us who to be, and second, we may find the information not to our liking.

Both outcomes lead to an identity crisis. Our interior worlds are no longer home, and the hostels created by the expectations of others are not sustainable. We have no place to linger. When this happens, we run the risk of falling into the depths of spiritual homelessness, as we feel perpetually victimized. We give away the power to create home as we walk away from our interior landscapes and sacrifice being internally referenced.

The loss of power leaves us with a small shelter. Seeing ourselves as victims, as people and events are less than supportive, leaves us ill equipped to make significant renovations to our psychic homes. Victims attempt to create sanctuary in a cavern of helplessness. This ailing attempt to create home will likely be reinforced by others. A few high-minded caretakers, determined to exercise their rescuing prowess, will convince anyone determined to be a victim that they are on the right path.

I am often reminded of Vladimir and Estragon, the two characters in Beckett's play *Waiting For Godot*. They wait onstage for the arrival of Monsieur Godot, whose arrival will transform their lives. Their patience is not rewarded, as Monsieur Godot never shows up. Is Beckett suggesting that home cannot be created for us by others? Can it be that it takes courage to stop waiting for Godot? Do we condemn ourselves to victimhood when we cannot exercise enough courage to stop waiting? Does the loss of courage lead to the homelessness of living like a victim? What are you waiting for?

Becoming the Victim

Victims define themselves as helpless when it comes to responding to life's challenges. They possess a propensity to view life as doing them in and to view themselves as unable to bring meaning and fulfillment to their lived experience. They are literally not home in their lives. Their lives do not belong to them. They are homeless.

There are at least four alleged benefits to the homelessness that happens to those who define themselves as victims. The first is that because they define themselves as powerless, they think they have no responsibility for what happens to them. Of course, in the normal course of events, they will be perpetrators of acts resulting from their ordinary human shortcomings. When they create some form of harm or discord, they immediately declare themselves the victim of the situation, making sure to circumvent self-accountability. Second, since victims will not save themselves, they entitle themselves to be saved by others. They easily slip into self-righteousness as they assess how effective others are at doing the saving. Third, because they allegedly have no power, victims can remain conveniently risk avoidant. And fourth, victims are exempt from living life on life's terms. Instead, they get to protest the awful events happening to them and how much is out of their control.

Victims wander aimlessly. Our longing and our wills position us somewhere; longing reflects a deep direction of the heart while the will sets some intention into motion. Victims implicitly define themselves as too small to adequately embark upon life's journey. They have an adversarial relationship with life, refusing to take up residency in what fate offers them.

Forever Rightsizing

Refusing to commit to *rightsizing* ourselves is another attitude that leaves us self-alienated and homeless. It is too easy to make ourselves either undersized or oversized, leaving us in the grip of either false modesty or arrogance.

Paul Coelho said, "Let us be absolutely clear about one thing: we must not confuse humility with false modesty or servility." We can think of humility as graciously accepting our limits, while false modesty deflates our gifts, talents, and natural abilities. With false modesty, we pretend we are smaller than we actually are. Such pretense has several presumed benefits, similar to the victim's. *Undersizing* ourselves may be an attempt to communicate to others that we are not a threat and that we are therefore deserving of their acceptance. We can also feign less-than-adequate capability in order to avoid either taking responsibility or embarking upon some risk. Also, false modesty is often an attempt to overcorrect and avoid arrogance.

For example, a heavy price was paid in my family of origin for any statement sounding boastful. Shame would quickly shower down on anyone attempting to bring attention to an achievement or some success. I learned to downplay any accomplishment or skill of my own. Initially, I was hiding the excitement and fulfillment of my athletic and academic endeavors. However, soon I became a refugee, driven from the homeland of my soul. In junior high school, I would be confused about how a girl came to have a crush on me or why I was given an athletic award. Later, in college, I recall being stopped by my ethics professor, who wanted to know if I had yet applied to study philosophy in graduate school. I was confused by his implicit confidence in my ability to undertake graduate study. I had taken great solace in defending myself against any accusation of being arrogant. I no longer knew my gifts, unable to distinguish my strengths from my weaknesses. And like any good falsely modest person, I was waiting for Godot to arrive, to let me know that I possessed some level of worth, even if such an announcement would confuse me.

And of course, there was the occasional unconscious swing into arrogance, in which I attempted to inoculate myself against the self-loathing bred from my false modesty. But as Edmund Burke said, "Whoever undertakes to set himself up as a judge of Truth and Knowledge is shipwrecked by the laughter of the gods." Arrogance is an inflation; as we set ourselves up as a source of truth and knowledge, we scurry away from our limits and shortcomings. When we pretend we are bigger than we actually are, we play charades, acting like a genuine person. The best we can hope is that someone will be impressed enough to help massage our self-contempt, which our arrogance is compensating for.

The arrogant inflation allegedly uplifts us, distancing us from what we deem common and parochial. This temporary lift is another attempt at comforting us, given the disdain we hold for ourselves. However, we do not live comfortably in arrogance, as we inevitably fall back into the reality of ourselves, confronted once more by the travail of hoisting ourselves out of the human condition again and again.

While recently riding my bike through a neighboring town, I saw a young man whom I regularly see in the gym. Whenever I encounter him, I am struck by his body armor. His shoulders sit on each side of his head like two large stones, protecting the encampment of his face and head. When he walks, only his shoulders move back and forth—collapsing forward a bit, appearing to provide his heart with some shielding. Although he is thirtysomething, he wears attire more fitting for a young teenager. When I pass him in the gym, I temporarily lose my breath and imagine some form of violation that possibly led to his fortification.

As I passed him on my bicycle, I again experienced a shallowness of breath, accompanied by a familiar sympathy. However, as I approached the upcoming hill, I was aware of a smile on my face. I became instantly curious about this misplaced smirk. And as quickly, I bumped into an arrogance lifting me up and away from the well-garrisoned young man on the sidewalk.

I impressed myself with my ability to camouflage my emotional injuries. Unlike this hulk of a man, my persona suggested something more gentle and unaffected. Was I actually taking pride in the incongruence between my inner and outer worlds? Could I actually think I was somehow better than the young man sporting his physical safeguards? Didn't I also have my protective devices? Was I willing to continue to applaud myself for concealing my citadel? After advancing several miles on my bicycle, I began to see the young man as a muse, calling me to more clarity regarding my arrogance.

Rightsizing is not something we arrive at; we need always to remain students of it. Becoming curious about a number of things will help us to move in this direction:

- Do I compare and contrast myself with others, with confirmation of my own inferiority being the inevitable conclusion?
- Do I compare and contrast myself with others, with confirmation of my own superiority being the inevitable conclusion?
- Am I aware of my gifts, talents, or innate skills?
- Do I typically find the gifts of others inadequate or not measuring up?
- Is it challenging for me to receive a compliment?
- Do I customarily work alone, seeing no need for collaboration?
- Am I susceptible to waving the banners of my accomplishments?
- Do I regularly acknowledge others for their contributions?
- Am I confused about how others have benefited from my contributions?
- Do I worry about getting enough attention?

A Homeless Heart

When we are consistently oversized or undersized, we struggle to find home within our own hearts. Leaving our hearts is a strong expression of being emotionally displaced. This wandering is not typically provoked by something sweet but rather by some violation or threat. The milder versions of vacating the heart are reflected by a number of defensive postures aimed at protecting our hearts. We become heart-absent by numbing enough, distracting enough, and moving fast enough.

I recently noticed my own fast moves aimed at protecting my heart. I had just finished having dinner with a young man whom I previously mentored and had not seen in quite a while. As we exited the restaurant, he paused, made eye contact, and said, "I really love you."

Before I could take a breath, I replied, "I love you too," the words moving with exceptional velocity. The quickness of my reply appeared to have palpable force aimed at intercepting the energy of his expression before it could reach my body.

Several hours later, I became more curious about my rapid response. Did his message stir some unexpected heart opening in me? Did I feel vulnerable as the recipient of an expression of this man's love? Feeling vulnerable seems to accompany some unexpected opening of heart. My hunch is that if we did not feel vulnerable when our hearts open, we likely would not feel the need to protect them.

What is the vulnerability of a heart opening all about? This poem expresses it well:

> All things penetrate the heart of a child.
> Tenderness, warmth, welcome and joy
> easily find their way into the heart of a child.
> So does harm, disgust, venom and rejection
> find some porous opening into the heart

of a child. When something cold and dark finds its
way into the heart of a child, that child decides
she is unlovable. And unlovable means discardable.

Being discarded ushers in the possibility of dying.
And so the heart remembers many years later,
being penetrated might mean dying and there lies
the depths of our feeling vulnerable.
(Anonymous)

From this passage, we can see why we feel vulnerable when our hearts
open. There is an old feeling of vulnerability held as a heart memory.
This is a bodily knowing that an open heart can be penetrated by
actions and/or words, suggesting we are unlovable and therefore face
the possibility of banishment. The homeless heart takes no chances.
It closes and hardens, protecting against whatever may seek entry—
good or bad. This heart has learned to trust only its locked doors in
the name of survival.

However, a homeless heart is without occupancy, unlived,
enduring a slow death in the name of securing survival. The warmth
and love offered to us is cordially acknowledged and never allowed in.

Alienated from Others

Another way that we find ourselves spiritually homeless is to alienate
ourselves from others. As John O'Donohue said, "Nothing in creation
is ever totally at home in itself." This is in keeping with the thinking
of mystics from every spiritual tradition. That is, home happens as
we unite with something larger than us. It is easy to drift away from
feeling truly known and understood or even wanting to be known.
But others can make a significant contribution to helping us create
home.

However, honoring the diversity of beliefs and values held by us and our significant others is critical. We will always witness family members, friends, and colleagues making choices we would not endorse. Being in the presence of significant difference evokes tension and feelings of helplessness that become critical to accept if we are to support our rapport with other folks.

Typically there are six ways in which we alienate ourselves from others. The first is being unaccepting of our helplessness to change others and therefore alienating them by demanding that they be different. The second is having weak boundaries, which allows others to define us and typically causes us to avoid others to secure who we are. The third is not knowing how to make requests in support of what we want from others. The fourth is adhering rigidly to a role, not allowing our desires and values to define how we interact. The fifth is attempting to avoid being hurt when hurt is inevitable, as in a committed relationship. Sixth and last is withdrawing inwardly so that we remain anonymous to others. We examine each of these six methods of self-alienation in the sections below.

Helplessness

We are not taught to feel and accept the helplessness associated with our closest relationships. When feeling helpless cannot be tolerated, we move into overt and covert strategies aimed at influencing others. These tactics typically lead to greater alienation. Those we are attempting to convert might succumb to our maneuvers, sacrificing their uniqueness and becoming faithful converts. However, as extensions of us, they have not truly joined us because their core is absent.

The second reaction to our attempts at colonization may be rebellion and resentment by others. They move further away from us, attempting to safeguard their individuality. Homelessness is heightened as we send the message, "Your uniqueness will not be honored here." Alienation is often the result of persistent attempts to control others in the name of offering them some much needed assistance.

Attempting to control others is commonly portrayed as an act of altruism enacted for their benefit. The unspoken truth is that the person attempting to influence is seeking some level of satisfaction. A father moves into a strong advisory capacity with his adult children. His unsolicited recommendations are met with distancing as he attempts to secure redemption for the guilt of not having been as available in their childhoods as he would have hoped. A husband begins to hide his wife's liquor when he decides her drinking is getting out of hand. He likely lives from the illusion that his spousal responsibility is to save her from her alcoholism. His refusal to accept his powerlessness reflects the internal mandate that her drinking reflects some failure of his loving. The weakness of his boundaries blurs his vision as to where he ends and she begins.

Weak Boundaries

A weak boundary is reflected in an inability to say *yes* and *no* authentically. Our boundaries are compromised by excessive accommodation, pleasing, avoiding conflict, and attachment to seeking approval. When *yes* and *no* are less than genuine, we become alienated in a crevice of distorted truth. Poor boundaries guarantee spiritual homelessness.

Requests

We are not taught that we should clearly represent our needs and desires by making clear, concrete requests. Typically, we do not simply ignore our desires but rather move into the employment of manipulative schemes in order to get what we want.

I recently heard Justin, a retired teacher, offer an account of what he did throughout his life in order to get his needs met.

"I belong to a men's support group that meets weekly. We had planned to hike a nearby mountain, but I didn't attend our meeting the week before the hike was to take place—when the group changed the date of the hike. I arrived at the designated meeting place prepared for the hike only to discover there was no hike. When I returned to the group the following week, I expressed to the men how angry and violated I felt.

"I appreciated how heard I felt by the men as they offered no excuses for forgetting me. However, as the days passed, I became increasingly curious about the deep feeling of being violated, which I could not release. It just seemed to be a bit over the top, given the situation. I mean, I had been inconvenienced, but I had not experienced any significant loss—so it was odd that the feeling of violation weighed heavy on my chest.

"I became aware of how difficult it is for me to identify what I want from others, therefore making it extremely difficult to formulate any clear requests. However, it has always been very easy for me to attend to the needs of others, even anticipating what might best serve them. Could it be that I had been making covert deals along the way? These deals might sound like 'I dedicate myself to acknowledging and responding to your needs favorably. I expect you to meet my needs as recompense for what I have done for you.'

"When I imagined these covert deals showing up as a written contract I made with the men in the group, I saw only my name on the dotted line. I then knew that all previous contracts were endorsed only by me. I also knew that the feeling of having been violated was more related to the alleged contract than to actually being forgotten at the mountain. As I looked closer at all of this, I realized that as a kid, I had dismissed my needs in order not to burden my parents. I decided to begin taking my needs more seriously. I might feel more at home now as I make requests of the men who support me."

Justin gleaned important insights about the absence of requests and his alienation from others. He was willing to fumble, attempting to give a clear voice to what he was wanting and feeling the fear that men might feel burdened by his requests and reject him.

Roles

Roles are fundamentally socially prescribed ways of talking and acting. These prescriptions are useful, seductive, and dangerous. They offer practical ways to participate in social organizations and institutions. We can see them as maps offering direction: how to act as a teacher, parent, nurse, entrepreneur, etc. They make it possible not to have to reinvent the wheel as we step into preordained roles.

The seduction and danger of roles is that they can easily be substituted for genuine personal identity. Roles can be very attractive borrowed identities for folks who grew up in highly dysfunctional and chaotic families. These people find relief in being able to identify what is an appropriate and acceptable way to act. Once they know what is valued, they often become high achievers. The dilemma is that they are simply taking sanctuary in a hostel and not the home of authenticity.

It is only too easy for us to relate to each other by relating from role to role, or from one function to another function. These functions are institutionally formulated in support of the institution's mission. The illusion is that safety and meaning come to us as we take up residency in a role. However, we stop relating heart to heart, and emotional isolation begins to build, ushering in homelessness. We no longer engage with authentic words that carry our sorrow, longing, fear, and love. Greetings like "How are you?" are empty words void of an honest interest. When we engage role-to-role long enough, our homelessness deepens as we begin to believe we are the fabric of our roles rather than the soul within.

Hurt

We are not taught how to be emotionally hurt, such that we can sustain a meaningful rapport while feeling hurt. Several choices we commonly make when we are hurt foster alienation. The first choice is to deny hurt feelings, pretending they don't exist, or to fire up with anger instead. Feeling hurt is typically accompanied by feeling vulnerable, which can add to the weight of the denial.

Second, if we feel the hurt, we can easily slip into defining ourselves as victims. Self-righteousness often travels with defining ourselves as victims. Victims claim to be above reproach and immune to enacting upon another the harm they themselves have endured. From their self-righteous posture, it becomes easy to build a moral case against the character of the perpetrator. With the perpetrator duly accused, we can easily move into a story that any good relationship should not be susceptible to such pain.

Our stories move us further and further away from the alleged perpetrator as we attempt to distract from feeling the hurt. We are at home neither with the other nor ourselves.

Stuck Inside

We have seen that we become homeless by getting excessively externally referenced. From such a position, we remain foreigners to our own interior landscape. However, we can also take up quarters internally, forgetting that we can never be totally at home within ourselves. Home is an act of co-creation.

In his book *The Seventh Solitude*, Ralph Harper describes the Danish philosopher Kierkegaard: "Kierkegaard journeyed to the interior and never came back." Introverts are likely more susceptible to journeying to the interior and not coming back. What is the seduction pulling us away from the world? What does it mean not to come back?

We might say that the seduction is a promise to be able to return to the womb. We withdraw into the sanctuary and emptiness of our own beliefs, feelings, longings, and imaginings. The temptation is the lure of gaining an alleged control over our destiny. There is a refusal to live life on life's terms, convinced that the gods need not have the last say. We fall prey to the distortion that we can have home without being touched, moved, disappointed, angered, and inspired by the vision and choices of others.

It can be only too easy to build a case against allowing ourselves to be impacted by others. We can cite their moral decrepitude, lack of inspiration, insensitivity, and stupidity as reasons to avoid taking risks in the external world. However, without the courage to take such risks, we cannot co-create home as we condemn ourselves to lose others and eventually lose ourselves.

The following passage from Nietzsche captures being driven and lost in the interior world: "Alone, I confront a tremendous problem. It is a forest in which I lose myself—a virgin forest. I need help. I need disciples. I need a master. To obey would be sweet! If I had lost myself on a mountain, I would obey the men who knew that mountain. . . And if I should meet a man capable of enlightening me on moral ideas, I would listen to him, I would follow him. But I find no one, no disciples, and fewer masters . . . I am alone."

It may be that without the resolve to accept the inevitability of being disappointed, we easily stumble into an arrogance guaranteeing isolation from others and ultimately from ourselves. Lost in the interior forest, we will not know what it truly means to give and receive love. We will not know home.

Alienated from Nature

As we technologize and urbanize the planet, it becomes easy to forget that Nature is our home. Spiritual homelessness often ensues as we move away from the forests, the mountains, and the seas. We have significantly severed our relationship with Nature, forgetting that Nature is our nature, its clay the primordial ooze of our DNA. Certainly, greed has called us to exploit the bounty of Nature without consideration for replenishing what we take. Reflective of our negligence is the destruction of the rainforest, unbridled carbon emissions, a dumping site in the Pacific Ocean the size of Texas, and the fact that 50 percent of animal and vegetable species have become extinct. Ernest Becker has suggested that there may be an arrogant compensation at play, putting us in an adversarial relationship with Nature:

> That man wants above all to endure and prosper, to achieve immortality in some way. Because he knows he is mortal, the thing he wants to do most is to deny this mortality. Mortality is connected to the natural, animal side of his existence; and so man reaches beyond and away from that side. So much so that he tries to deny it completely. As soon as man reached new historical forms of power, he turned against the animals with whom he had previously identified—with a vengeance, we now see, because animals embodied what man feared most, a nameless and faceless death.

Becker suggests that because of our technology and advanced weaponry, we set out to prove we had more control over death than did animals. This drive to deny our mortality begins to tear away at the very fabric of planet Earth as our home. We treat the Earth like drunken college students on spring break, with no care about how we befoul the ground beneath our feet. We unleash an insatiable desire to pleasure our senses in as many ways as possible, taking no notice of the inevitable losses, pretending we are not home—home being a place deserving of our attention to beauty and order.

When we lose gratitude for the gifts of Nature, unable to witness its beauty and unwilling to take stewardship for Nature, we are spiritually homeless. The more distant we are from Nature, the more distant we are from ourselves.

Einstein said, "Our task must be to free ourselves by widening our circle of compassion to embrace all living creatures and the whole of Nature and its beauty." The story of Lawrence Anthony, a conservationist in South Africa, reflects the task Einstein references. In 1999, Anthony rescued and rehabilitated a group of wild South African elephants that had been identified as dangerous. When Anthony died in March 2014, the elephants he had supported traveled for miles until reaching Anthony's home, where they stood in apparent vigil for two days in honor of the man who had cared for them.

Alienated from the Divine

> *It may be a species of impudence to think that the way you understand God is the way God is.*
> —Joseph Campbell

Campbell reminds us that our best attempts at defining God will fall very short. In fact, our determination to capture God in a bottle or in a book may condemn us to be alienated from the Divine. The ego protests the depth of mystery presented by the Divine. The ego is determined to issue an edict defining God. If the theological proclamation is driven by enough fear and self-adulation, then other religious perspectives will likely be viewed as idolatrous. Spiritual homelessness is heightened as tolerance for different religious views is expunged.

An old definition of the word *idolatry* is "that which does not deserve my respect and reverence." The opposite of idolatry would be a willingness to remain devotionally curious about what truly deserves respect and reverence. The ego wants to substitute how right it is for remaining curious. Hence, the ego does not surrender graciously to the mystery of the Divine. As Thomas Moore said, "This is one of the main differences in the new personal religion: going deep rather than being right."

Left to the ego's attachment to being right, we lose depth and a home in the mystery of the Divine. It can be extremely seductive to the ego to ignore creating home with the mysteries of the self, others, and Nature. Why waste time with these three expressions of mystery when we can pretend to directly access the Almighty! What a delight it can be to employ the camouflage offered by the ethereal nature of the Divine, allowing the ego to decide on whatever meets its fancy when it comes to defining God. There may be no greater idolatry than to decide that the three manifestations of the Divine (we, others, and Nature) are not worth our time and energy.

The Anglican mystic Julian of Norwich suggested, "And when we know and see truly and clearly what our self is, then shall we truly and clearly know our Lord God in fullness of joy." The Hasidic mystic Martin Buber claimed, "When two people relate to each other authentically and humanly, God is the electricity that surges between them." Francis of Assisi reminds us of the connection between Nature and the Divine: "If you have men who will exclude any of God's creatures from the shelter of compassion and pity, you will have men who will deal likewise with their fellow men."

Spiritual homelessness is inevitable if we ignore the religious call to healing. The word *religion* means "reconnecting, putting back together," meaning reconnecting to ourselves, others, Nature, and the Divine. We, others, and Nature can be seen as the down-and-dirty of religion. If we dare to reconnect to these three expressions of the Divine, then we are compelled to undertake an arduous psychological and spiritual task.

Can we find enough courage and compassion to reconnect to what we have banished within ourselves? Can we allow ourselves to accept being self-righteous, arrogant, falsely modest, and insensitive? Or can we reclaim some skill or ability we denied because it made someone we care about uncomfortable? Can we eliminate or diminish the dynamics of "right-wrong" and "win-lose" as we relate to others? Can we find space in our beliefs for those who think and act differently from us? Can we see biases and prejudices we possess and the fear that drives them? Can we find enough grace and gratitude to honor our kinship with all living things? Can we find the wisdom that suggests upon our deathbed we will not take what we have consumed but leave what we have given?

Holding or regaining an authentic vision of home calls for an understanding of and commitment to presence. When seekers are short on presence, their quest urges them out of the moment, not allowing for a well-informed present. Restlessness can drive seekers away from themselves and what is immediately available. Hence, making sense of presence becomes a valued spiritual practice. We will explore the idea of presence in the next chapter.

A Blessing for Spiritual Homelessness

You were always destined to go home, again and again. This going home is about both the arrival and the pilgrimage. It is a place outside of you and inside of you. It must be a place where safety and rest are provided by forces preventing darkness from penetrating. A place where you remember who you are—held, encouraged, and nurtured by warmth and beauty.

Sensually know the tension between stillness and movement. Surrender to the tautness that asks for a reprieve from an extended stay or from an agitation that takes you away from yourself. Allow the senses to be filled with the welcome of a new dawn and quieted by the blanket of dusk, content to allow your longing to rest. Find the faith that you will be held throughout the night.

You are kin to a sublime restlessness. This unease is a friend, calling you to the sacred. From this place a fire burns in you, determined to illuminate the sustainable. The hollowness of popular seductions is revealed. You hear the call to something in vogue, but your restlessness has brought you to these places before. You know how amenable your ego can be to these titillating gyrations.

Your heart is less at home when called away from itself for some fleeting repose meant only to distract from what calls to you. A well-worn armament provides inadequate space for the largeness of your heart. You are willing now to be penetrated, allowing for a full breath of vulnerability.

You have come to know this life and this life knows you. You've befriended risks, knowing how to fear and how to be hurt.

You know now that homelessness is either being lost outside or lost in the forest inside. Each offers the illusion of home, and yet there is no hearth in either place without the other. And so you have learned to listen to a quiet voice telling you either to pull into some forgotten part of yourself or to stand, taking some risk that life has requested.

3

Presence

Your hand opens and closes, opens and closes. If it were always a fist or always stretched open, you would be paralyzed. Your deepest presence is in every small contracting and expanding, the two as beautifully balanced and coordinated as birds' wings.

—Rumi

SEEKERS ARE ASKED TO REMAIN students of presence. It will take a kinship with presence to birth an intimate sensibility about what is and what might be. The more we can practice a sense of presence, the more we can discern what the threshold holds for us. Is what we seek already here? Do we need to prepare for a threshold crossing?

Presence is a way to connect to ourselves and to others. The chronic trauma expert Peter Levine offers some poignant themes about presence in a narrative found in his book *In an Unspoken Voice*. The story begins with Levine having just been struck by a vehicle as he was crossing the street. He lies in the street paralyzed and numb.

A paramedic approaches him and asks a series of questions, leaving Levine disoriented and confused. Levine finds his voice, imploring the paramedic to back off; the paramedic complies with his request. Shortly after, a young woman arrives offering a more contracted presence:

After a few minutes, a woman unobtrusively inserts herself and quietly sits by my side. "I'm a doctor, a pediatrician," she says. "Can I be of any help?" "Please just stay with me," I reply. Her simple, kind face seems supportive and calmly concerned. She takes my hand in hers, and I squeeze it. She gently returns the gesture. As my eyes reach for hers, I feel a tear form. The delicate and strangely familiar scent of her perfume tells me that I am not alone. A trembling wave of release moves through me, and I take my first deep breath. Then a jagged shudder of terror passes through my body. . .

In a little while, a softer trembling begins to replace the abrupt shudders. I feel alternating waves of fear and sorrow. . . . . A Slower breath brings me the scent of her perfume. Her continued presence sustains me. As I feel less overwhelmed, my fear softens and begins to subside.

Levine credits the young woman's presence with affording his body and emotions the opportunity to express their natural response to a traumatic incident. "I came through mercifully unscathed, both physically and emotionally," he writes.

This story points toward the power of a *contracted presence*, that is, one not loaded with excessive language and audacious, heroic action. What distinguishes the young woman's offering of presence from the paramedic's offering of presence? What made her offering so helpful and healing? In this chapter we will explore the difference between a contracted presence and absence, the difference between contracted and expanded presence, and how we can live with greater self-presence.

A Contracted Presence

Several elements of the contracted presence depicted in Levine's story are worth exploring. These features of a contracted presence tend to be countercultural. Although potent, they do not line up with our typical understanding of power, which is typically characterized by vigorous action and exemplified by the determination to effect some desired outcome. We are accustomed to understanding a sense of presence as an active participation in an event. However, we can think of a contracted presence as a passive participation. We must also consider other aspects of a contracted presence and the role of passive participation, such as absence, place of refuge, vulnerability, and whole-body listening.

Passive Participation

We can think of the young woman's contracted presence as a way of passively participating in an injured man's ordeal. Her *passive participation* is concentrated on Levine's experience rather than on her intervening with some skill or remedy. She arrives on the scene and turns control of what is to take place over to the wounded man in the street. She's willing to join the man, immobilized by suspending bold action. She moves into the power of surrender and the helplessness accompanying it. Ezra Bayde describes this as follows:

> We all dread the helplessness of losing control; yet real freedom lies in recognizing the futility of demanding that life be within our control. Instead, we must learn the willingness to feel—to say yes to—the experience of helplessness itself. This is one of the hidden gifts of serious illness and loss. It pushes us right to our edge, where we may have the good fortune to realize that

our only real option is to surrender to our experience
and let it just be.

When we have been acculturated with the importance of active
participation, it can be very difficult to appreciate the value of "letting
it just be." The ego is convinced that its preservation depends upon
taking the right action. It can be very challenging to surrender to
living in a larger story. In this larger narrative, we are not simply
impacting life with our wills but also remaining receptive to being
informed by life, even when the information does not support what
we want.

I regularly experience my resistance to passively participating in the
stories of two of my friends. One man struggles with a metastasizing
cancer, while the other man suffers with daily pain due to post-
polio syndrome (PPS). I am consistently convinced that my passive
participation is not enough, alerting me to how much I have deified
heroic action. I am just starting to understand that when I discredit
myself for not doing enough, I obstruct an offering of contracted
presence. I can also remind myself that my feelings of helplessness
only pertain to some overt action. I am not helpless regarding being
willing to learn about the benefits of offering contracted presence. I
can begin to passively participate by unobtrusively inserting myself,
sitting by their sides and introducing an important absence.

Absence

The *absence* of additional action is a big deal. It suggests that for the
moment, nothing else matters but the other's experience. We bring
no interesting intellectual material, no needs of our own, and no plan
of action. That is, nothing is introduced that could possibly compete
with the feelings and needs of the other person. Levine reports that the
combination of the young woman's gaze, her scent, and her squeezing

of his hand suggested to him that he was not alone. The absence of overt action in this case allowed for something softer and more hidden to surface. She authentically joined his reality and his experience of shock, terror, sorrow, and helplessness as he lay in the street. Deep feelings of helplessness brought the two strangers together: one's helplessness due to an accident and the other's helplessness due to the enormity of the task before her.

There is also the absence of an opportunity for Levine to have some rational explanation of her presence. Her offering is not an act of recompense for some kindness Levine previously gave her. Nor is Levine's deservedness of her giving based upon some mastery or achievement of his. His deservedness is grounded simply in being a fellow human being in need. I imagine a deep, soulful sigh in Levine's being, a temporary letting go of the hope that he could do enough to warrant such caring attention.

This kind of deservedness lies deep and hidden for most of us. There is an absence of control over making it happen because we have done neat stuff. In place of control is an emptiness that may be able to receive an act of kindness in a new way. No longer is there a mapping to something said or done, something possibly impressive; now there is only the wonder and beauty of kindness.

The power of the young woman's passive participation and contracted presence is further illustrated even in her physical absence. Levine writes: "As I am lifted into the ambulance, I close my eyes for the first time. A vague scent of the woman's perfume and the look of her quiet, kind eyes linger. Again, I have that comforting feeling of being held by her presence."

A very old definition of the word *hold* is "a place of refuge." We can say that the young woman's contracted presence was a place of refuge for Levine, even in her physical absence.

Place of Refuge

What exactly was this place of refuge offered by the young woman's contracted presence? Although Levine's story is more dramatic than most of our daily experiences, we can in varying degrees offer a place of refuge to those whom we encounter. Again, Levine says he is held by her presence. What exactly holds him, offering a place of refuge?

Henry James said, "Three things in human life are important: the first is to be kind; the second is to be kind; and the third is to be kind."

We can say that Levine is held by at least four levels of the woman's kindness. The first is the kindness that brings her to his side, as she is willing to interrupt her original plans. The second is the gentle communication that only his present situation really matters. She comes with no agenda. Arriving in this manner offers him an immense welcome. The ego is so accustomed to tracking the welcome we receive to some achievement or contribution we've made, thus confirming our entitlement to the welcome. This welcome is not dependent upon some prior liaison or rapport. In Levine's case, his brokenness and his humanity are welcomed just as a parent would welcome her newborn baby before the vernix is wiped from his body. There is an unequivocal purity about such a welcome. The third expression of kindness is her willingness to feel helpless and vulnerable with him. The fourth element of kindness is her willingness to remain with him until more help comes.

Vulnerability

An old definition of the word *vulnerable* is "able to be wounded." When we are not able to be wounded, we are likely so effectively garrisoned against threats that we also cannot feel loved, welcomed, desired, respected, and supported. Being wounded refers to feeling hurt, rejected, dismissed, criticized, and blamed, though not in danger of losing a limb.

As children, our experience of feeling vulnerable easily translates into "I am vulnerable and unsafe." When children feel shamed or ridiculed, it is not simply about being emotionally hurt; it's bigger than that. They understand being shamed as being unlovable and therefore at risk of being abandoned. It is the threat of being abandoned that creates the original fear of not being able to survive on one's own. Hence, for a child, feeling vulnerable means being vulnerable and therefore being in danger.

Vulnerability means being willing to practice feeling vulnerable and possibly being emotionally hurt, yet able to believe we can be lovable without forthcoming abandonment and death. It means becoming effective at distinguishing feeling vulnerable from being vulnerable—although there may always be some haunting of possible demise when we feel vulnerable. Being trapped in a burning building, being about to have an automobile accident, getting mugged, or being victimized by a home invasion are all examples of not only feeling vulnerable but also being vulnerable. But while being vulnerable threatens some physical injury or even our lives, feeling vulnerable allows us to be fully alive. As Brené Brown puts it, "Vulnerability is the birthplace of love, belonging, joy, courage, empathy, and creativity. It is the source of hope, empathy, accountability, and authenticity. If we want greater clarity in our purpose or deeper and more meaningful spiritual lives, vulnerability is the path."

The willingness to feel vulnerable allows us to be penetrated by love, which can be given and taken away. We feel a welcomed and also deeply forgotten. We feel the unease of stepping across a threshold and into a risky situation, and we also feel the satisfaction of having exercised enough courage to take that risk. Feeling vulnerable allows us to passively participate in life, supporting a contracted presence.

Whole-Body Listening

Listening with our whole body is an essential ingredient to a contracted presence and passive participation. Many years ago I was leading a communication training for foster grandparents. I paired up the participants—one speaking, the other listening without speaking for two minutes. Upon the conclusion of the first round, a woman in the speaker's role began sobbing uncontrollably. Her emotional response surprised me since the assigned topic was relatively innocuous.

I turned toward her and said, "Tell me what touches you so."

After gathering her breath, she explained, "I have not received ten seconds of uninterrupted attention in over sixty years and just got two whole minutes."

She was teaching the group more about the power of listening than I could ever have explained in a presentation.

What does it mean to enroll our bodies in the skill of listening? It mostly means to clear our minds by focusing on our breath—allowing our bodies to respond to the listener with different areas of tightness, stiffness, twitching, relaxation, or a need to contract or stretch. When we clear our minds from some preparation to respond verbally, our breath invites our body to receive the verbal and nonverbal energies of the speaker. This lack of verbal response, coupled with a soft, focused attention, energizes our presence. There is only one thing being attended to by the listener: the thoughts and feelings of the speaker.

Jon Kabat-Zenn, a teacher of mindfulness, reported this kind of experience when talking with the Dalai Lama, saying "You know when talking with him, it feels like he's really there with you, with genuine interest in the moment—not scanning the room for a better networking opportunity."

Whenever there is an urgency to speak, we can come back to the breath and quietly ask ourselves, "What else is here?" The ego motivates us to speak as if it knows exactly what is here, denying the depth of mystery surrounding what was said.

Although I have been practicing whole-body listening for some time, I inevitably find myself pressed to speak. It can be helpful to identify how we push ourselves toward speaking. My urgency to talk can be easily activated by a need to demonstrate I know something. Sometimes it's a need to interrupt the discomfort I feel due to what I am hearing. For example, I was recently listening to a friend describe his experience of attending a film alone and the shame he started to feel when a family he knew sat several rows in front of him. He did not want them to notice he was alone. As the film ended he vaulted himself abruptly out of the theater in the hope of not being noticed by his friends. I could feel my discomfort as I reflected on how I have successfully avoided attending a film alone. I returned to my breath and spoke when my friend appeared ready to hear me.

More than not, my dire need to speak is fueled by the distortion that what I have to say will be helpful and that the speaker is certainly eager to be helped by me. This aggrandizement of myself as a valuable resource is definitely in need of rightsizing.

Whole-body listening is mostly an invitation to use more than our head in order to listen. A contracted presence becomes rich with the reminder that what we are hearing is a large story containing many unknowns. Our immediate interpretations might be aimed at being impressive, and they can easily cut us off from the larger narrative. If we can return to the breath, then it is likely that more of these unknowns will be revealed. Oftentimes when I verbally acknowledge what I'm hearing, the speaker will credit me with an astute intuition. As much as I am flattered by the compliment, I am often simply reflecting back what my non-interrupting listening allowed me to hear.

A Contracted Absence

As much as we can create a contracted presence, we can also generate a *contracted absence*. Typically, introverts have an innate ability to create such an absence. They quietly and internally process what they believe, feel, and desire. Introverts learn early in life that they can cope with the demands, neglect, and possible abuse of childhood by boosting their introversion into anonymity. They can easily transform their quiet consideration of ideas into a sanctuary of anonymity, aimed at protecting themselves from criticism and ridicule. Their motto is: "If you can't see me, you can't get me." Parents may even experience the anonymity of the introverted child as a convenience, as this type of child is so much less demanding and intrusive.

However, it is common for introverted children to become not only anonymous to others but over time, to become anonymous to themselves. This inability to see their own emotions and preferences reduces tension. They no longer need to feel the strain of knowing how they feel—desiring to be heard and understood, they nevertheless choose to keep themselves a secret. The pressure is gone. They no longer know what they are hiding from the world.

In order to move out of a contracted absence, introverts need to learn how to discerningly protect themselves with anonymity as well as employ other forms of safeguards. Being an introvert myself, I have often been described as mysterious. The key for me is to be intentional about utilizing a cloaking device and clear about what's gained and what's lost in appearing mysterious. Sometimes, the feedback I received about my anonymity was actually about the other person's simply wanting more information than I was prepared to offer. Other times, I was excessively mysterious when I really wanted to be seen and included.

Forms of shielding that introverts can add to their self-care repertoire include making clear requests, employing effective boundaries, and confronting unacceptable behavior. The key is for them to honor their introversion without unconsciously amplifying it into anonymity, guaranteeing a contracted absence.

Expanded Presence

> *All growth is the desire of the soul to refine and enlarge its presence.*
>
> —John O'Donohue

When our presence is expanded, more of our energies are expressed. An *expanded presence* involves having more voice and/or exercising more action. We live in an extroverted society where verbosity and unbridled action are often revered. We marvel at a performance of multitasking, likely not noticing how much presence has been sacrificed. Hyperactivity spoken or acted springs us into the future. We hurriedly move into the next moment with exuberance, disabling our ability to settle into an authentic presence in the here and now.

Without discernment, our voice and our action can be an avalanche of sound and motion, signifying little. Here are some discerning questions that can help: Am I taking in a full breath as I speak? Does my pace allow the other to genuinely engage me? As I speak or act, am I able to have some sense of the impact my action has on the other? Am I aware of what is motivating me to speak or act? Does my pace allow me to remain in the here and now?

Our voice and our action will reflect an expanded presence if we speak and act in the present. It is often suggested that any semblance of personal power can only happen in the present. Since the past is complete and the future has not yet happened, it makes a good deal of sense to propose that our choices have their greatest degree of potency in the here and now.

However, it is unlikely that many of us avoid living in the present because we prefer losing power. The present is not only the place where power can take place; it is also where we get hurt and feel that hurt. Hence, again we are reminded of the value of allowing ourselves to feel vulnerable. Without it, we will not likely develop a kinship with the here and now, nor will we find the courage to have an authentic voice. An expanded presence happens when we have an authentic voice employing embodied language. Such language possesses elements of earth, fire, and water, all of which we'll discuss in this section.

In an Authentic Voice

> *When you give yourself permission to communicate what matters to you in every situation, you will have peace despite rejection or disapproval. Putting a voice to your soul helps you to let go of the negative energy of fear and regret.*
>
> —Shannon L. Alder

A voice reflecting an expanded presence must be authentic. An old meaning of the word *authentic* is "acting on one's own authority." Notwithstanding the power of genes and environment, an authentic voice reflects the speaker's taking his or her inner world very seriously. Although he's influenced by what's around him, he has little interest in drinking from the waters of popular belief. There is a deep investment in experiencing external attitudes as a muse arousing some personal vision. These awakening sensibilities may have been said before, but not quite in the same way. The authentic voice reflects the unique path of the speaker. It is a voice refusing to take refuge in either silence or the employment of clichés.

The courage of an authentic voice reflects the willingness to step away from anonymity. I recently heard a young man say, "Oh my God, getting authentic means I have to want to know me, accept me, and then take the risk to let you know me!" The young man was right. Acquiring an authentic voice is a big deal. We do not simply get such a voice; we must devote ourselves to deepening our capacity to speak from the authority of what we love, what we have lost, and what we have learned. Of course, an authentic voice must be guided by discernment if we are to avoid reducing our verbal utterances to something juvenile.

This is unlike what happens in Moliere's play *The Misanthrope*, when the principal character, Alceste, decides to entitle himself to an unrestricted display of his thoughts and feelings, resulting in farce and hilarity meant to entertain. We, on the other hand, must learn to bring discernment and compassion to our voices. Otherwise, we will likely generate excessive drama and farce, which are better kept in the hands of the playwright. Some discerning questions that can help bring compassion and clarity to an authentic voice include: Do I have a hidden agenda? What do I really want? How am I feeling emotionally? Is there anything I fear? What language best describes something about me, rather than mostly about others? Do I have some request that needs to be spoken?

Embodied Language

Embodied language has the power to penetrate our bodies. These words move and touch us; we are more able to hold what we are hearing. What is said is often heard as inspirational. The word *inspire* literally means "to breathe in." We take embodied language into our bodies.

The simplest examples of embodied language happen when we speak of desire, emotion, and passion. When we communicate one or more of these three energies, they can animate our bodies and arouse energies in our listeners. Our presence is expanded as our voices carry the uniqueness of our paths, our losses, our longings, our suffering, our defeats, and our victories.

If you desire to use more embodied language, then it will be important to let go of coded language. I recently witnessed a couple arguing, in the name of fairness and equity, about which of them had made greater contributions to their marriage. After listening to each of them suggest some contribution aimed at dropping more weight on his or her side of the scale, I offered that one or both of them might simply declare what they want more of. So they slowly loosened their grip on employing the code of fairness and said what they wanted more of.

We get good at talking in code because it brings a dimension of anonymity to our emotions and desires. We can probably handle people disagreeing with our ideas, but we might feel crushed if they laughed at our pain or told us that what we wanted was selfish or stupid. Any emotion or desire can be translated into coded categories such as morality, fairness, justice, religion, and what's reasonable or normal. Before our language can be embodied, we need to become effective at decoding our language and being able to speak the truth about how we feel, what we want, and what we are passionate about.

Earth, Fire, and Water

Embodied language predominately carries the elements of earth, fire, and water. The element of earth suggests clarity of focus, with reference to one or more of the five senses and actual behavior. Typically, language possessing earth is spoken more slowly, giving the speaker the opportunity to connect to the body through breath. When we bring earth energy to our language, our words take on sensuality, allowing them to be received by the whole body of the listener. There is ground holding this kind of language, allowing listeners to locate speakers whose vision can help them reorganize either the way they understand themselves or life—and join them if they desire. An example is the following excerpt from the poem "Second Sight":

Sometimes, you need the ocean light
and colors you've never seen before
painted through an evening sky.

Sometimes, you need your God
to be a simple invitation,
not a telling word of wisdom.

Sometimes, you need only the first shyness
that comes from being shown things
far beyond your understanding,

so that you can fly and become free
by being still and by being still here.

And then there are times you need to be
brought to ground by touch
and touch alone.
(David Whyte, "Second Sight")

The element of fire signifies passion, anger, longing, desire, and commitment. It often suggests the presence of biophilia, or a love of life. We incorporate it into our language by following D.H. Lawrence's admonition: "Be still when you have nothing to say; when genuine passion moves you, say what you've got to say, and say it hot." Fire language has the power to inspire by igniting new vision and motivation. Words of fire are great for reminding us of what's important to us, where our devotion and passion live. Often the germination of our values begins with our ability to speak with fire. The fire of anger has the power to incinerate resentment and self-pity. Similar to a lightning strike creating a forest fire that burns away dead vegetation, making space for new growth, the fire of our words can burn away worn-out beliefs. Ideas that no longer serve to invigorate stewardship for children, the elderly, the disenfranchised, and the environment can be scorched.

The element of water in our language reflects the presence of sorrow, grief, sadness, hurt, pain, and sometimes joy. Speaking from water allows us to grieve our losses. We can tell the stories of what dies, renewing our relationship to impermanence, allowing us to get more honest about life. There are also tears of joy where the water flows from streams of elation. When we allow water to flow through our words, we can wash over others with a stream of compassion and empathy.

Similar to the capacity of water to ionize air—diminishing airborne allergens, pathogens, and pollutants—the flow of tears can reduce pollutants in our psychic air, the home of our beliefs. Our emotional waters ionize our thinking, lessening our inclinations toward revenge, resentment, and self-loathing.

A stone that is washed ashore, leveled, and smoothed by the rushing waters of changing tides can speak to the power of water related to earth. Each time I hold such a stone, I feel the relationship this stone has had with water. Its edges have given way to a disk-shaped contour, smooth and inviting to the touch, telling the story of its intimate kinship with the movement of water. So it is with our own psychic rough edges. Our psyche's earth energy can harden, bringing rigidity and roughness to our choices and how we focus our attention. Routine behaviors become firm and inflexible, disallowing for exploration, adventure, and spontaneity. If our tears move like the tides, we can bring a softness to the contour of our words as they fall gently upon the ears of our listeners.

Embodied language imbued with earth, fire, and water can touch and move listeners. There is a possibility for co-creation, collaboration, awakening, and change. Embodied words communicate two very significant messages. The first is that the speaker is here and now, accessible to be engaged by the listener. The second is that the speaker has integrated the thoughts being communicated. The speaker is likely walking his or her talk, making what he or she is saying more believable and more trustworthy.

The very idea that we are employing verbal language suggests the presence of air (ideas, beliefs, opinions, recommendations). However, with inadequate earth, fire, or water, ideas typically generate more ideas (air), until the speaker's message eventually evaporates, sustaining little or no earthly relevance. If we don't know what an idea is asking us, then it is likely swollen with excessive air.

It is important to note that language inflated with lavish amounts of air can be seductive. Listeners commonly mistake imprudent amounts of air for intelligence. Speakers can seduce themselves into thinking that their ethereal attachments exempt them from taking risks. However, Hamlet's story reminds us that no matter how extensive our ruminations, an abundance of air will not make us immune from the perils of fate.

Expanded Absence

Extroverts are inclined to create an *expanded absence*. Extroverts use spoken language to determine what they feel and what they actually believe. As I listen to an extroverted friend speak, he often pauses and says, "You don't actually think that I believe anything I've said up to this point, do you?" He is reminding me that he is speaking out loud in order to clarify for himself what he thinks.

Extroverts figure out in childhood that if they say a lot and say it fast, it will be difficult for the listener to actually know what is being said. Hence, safety for extroverts happens as they take refuge behind a pile of words, which I often refer to as fog. Their motto is "You can't get me because I'm hiding behind a lot of stuff."

Unlike introverts, who run the risk of their contracted absence's making them look shy and unapproachable, the extrovert benefits from an extroverted culture's likely viewing their unrestrained use of language as a reflection of their being bright and congenial. The extrovert's expanded absence goes easily missed.

In order for extroverts to undo their fogging, they need to slow down their verbal delivery, breathe deeply, increase their mindfulness of how they feel in the moment, employ effective boundaries, and confront unacceptable behavior.

Receiving Presence

We have been looking at ways to offer presence and ways to generate absence. Now let's examine what it's like to receive presence.

What makes one person's offering of presence comforting and secure and another's invasive and uncomfortable? In Peter Levine's story, he did not want the expanded presence of the EMT but he did want the contracted presence of the young pediatrician. Another person in Levine's situation might have experienced the EMT's presence as supportive and reassuring. So learning what kind of offering of presence best serves us is a valuable lesson. To some degree, what works for us will be situational. Fundamentally, though, two factors determine what kind of presence works for us. The first is how we want to be joined by others. What kinds of energies serve as a conduit between others and us? Do we need something soft and gentle (contracted) or something spirited and dynamic (expanded)? Or do we need a combination of subdued and animated energy? The second determining element is how we might want to be empowered by others' presence. What do we want to be able to do or accomplish due to their presence?

Thomas, a young friend of mine, described a meeting with his mentor that characterized how different offerings of presence can work for a person.

"I had an important meeting with my mentor last week regarding family issues I'm struggling with," explained Thomas.

"I would like to hear about it. I know you appreciate the support Joe offers you," I responded.

"Well, as you know, I've been challenged by my aging father, who has never expressed an interest in knowing me, throughout my entire life," he said, with a note of hopelessness.

"Yes, I'm aware of the longevity of the estrangement between you and your father," I said.

"That has been exacerbated by my father's increased dementia. My daughter recently confirmed that her husband finds it threatening to be known by me and has little interest in knowing me. I told Joe [his mentor] that I had no idea how to best cope with these family matters," Thomas added.

"Was Joe helpful?" I asked.

"Well, that's just it. Joe said he felt sad to hear about the impact my father and son-in-law were having on me. He even shed a couple of tears. I could feel how deeply empathic he was with my situation. His response was kind of helpful, but not really. I mean, I knew he cared. But when I would later have to face these two family members, I would need more than Joe's caring," reported Thomas.

"Then what made the meeting so meaningful for you?" I asked.

"It was one word he repeated several times during our meeting: *separation*. I then knew I could separate from my father and from my son-in-law, and do it with less guilt. I gradually understood that I could separate *and* be kind when interacting with them. Somehow, my ability to be kind is connected to my feeling less guilty—and it's been working!" Thomas declared robustly.

"Was it really the one word you found helpful?" I asked.

"Yes. I found a new level of permission to separate from both of them. Joe is always convinced that if he exhibits enough empathy and sympathy, all will be well. I needed to figure out what to do with my father and son-in-law, and Joe's empathy was just not going to be enough to help me relate to them in a way that worked for me."

"What was Joe's response when you explained how much one word from him had done for you?"

"He was in disbelief. He was convinced that his unconditional acceptance of me was what empowered me. I pushed back and told Joe that if I had left our meeting with his acceptance only, I would have been more confused and disempowered than ever!"

Thomas' story illustrates several important characteristics of receiving presence. First, recipients know best what kind of offering of presence will work for them. Second, sometimes it is not enough to be joined in deep empathy; we need to receive some form of guidance supporting our empowerment to make choices that work for us. Third, when making an offering of presence, it's best not to be too attached to what we think is best for the recipient. And we saw in Levine's story just how important it is to refuse an offering of presence we know will not work for us.

Self-Presence

Understanding the quality and strength of someone's presence is to a great degree a reflection of our familiarity with our own sense of presence, especially the quality of presence we have with ourselves. Before we can understand how to bring a degree of depth to our presence, it may be helpful to explore how we move into creating absence.

The self is and remains an essential mystery, yet it is the fundamental focus for the seeker—the beginning place. Who we are continues to remain unfinished, no matter how much the ego insists that we are a finely tuned finished product. Therefore, follow John O'Donohue's advice: "Awaken to the mystery of being here and enter the quiet immensity of your own presence."

To do this, we need to remain committed to a self-examining life. From such a commitment, we can attend to the ongoing task of developing a *mindful self-presence*. This presence to the self happens by becoming an observer of our many different parts. However, before addressing what it takes to develop a mindful self-presence, we must examine another form of self-presence that I call *instinctual self-presence*. Elements of instinctual self-presence include increased mindfulness, learning how to be grounded, and developing a capacity to remain in the present while crafting an observer of the self. We'll discuss all of these concepts in the sections below.

Instinctual Self-Presence

Instinctual self-presence happens as we surrender to the instincts or wisdom of the body. It is extremely easy to forget about bodily wisdom, as so much of our lives happen from the chin up. We see, hear, smell, taste, talk, listen, breathe, and think with our head. How easy it is to forget about the rest of us, from our throat to our feet. It can be difficult to remember our whole bodies, as education and religion typically encourage us to be top-heavy. Early on, our bodies are defined as dirty, restless, disturbing, and invasive.

Ken Wilber says, "Few of us have lost our minds, but most of us have long ago lost our bodies." I periodically remind myself that one of my ancestors was the saber-toothed tiger, and that helps me to appreciate the instinctual knowing that lives in my body.

I received a valuable lesson years ago about instinctual presence while studying martial arts. Our sensei was customarily tolerant and encouraging, but every now and then he became irritated with what he perceived as sloppiness of form. When his irritation maxed out, he brought all activity in the dojo to a halt, demanding our attention. He would point to two students who were to square off and spar for two minutes—what must have felt like a lifetime of battle. He would proceed to drop a colorful sash indicating that the two fighters could commence and spar until a chime was struck two minutes later.

Although I had been studying martial arts for several years, I had successfully avoided this much-feared confrontation.

The second I knew our sensei was about to call for a sparring match, I quietly dropped into prayer—and in those days, I seldom prayed. I hoped not to face the strength and speed of any of the younger students, all of whom were twenty years younger than me. But one day my divine support came to an end, as the sensei pointed to the most skilled student in the class and then to me.

I quickly searched for an excuse, like a sore shoulder—anything to avoid my certain defeat and possible injury—but to no avail. I took a prepared position, with my knees bent, hands raised, all motivated by sheer terror. My plan was to bob and weave for two minutes, then maybe take a quick bathroom break. God willing, I would come out the other side in one piece.

The sash dropped, and my opponent moved in for the kill as I desperately attempted to remain just out of his reach. I was determined to give the appearance of actually being aggressively engaged while simply doing what I could to prevent myself from being hurt and humiliated. Suddenly, I heard the sound of the chime calling the confrontation to an obvious premature end. The sensei walked over to me, standing with his nose less than six inches from my nose.

"Do you actually believe you can outthink and anticipate where this young man will launch kicks and punches?" asked the sensei, with a note of condemnation, suggesting that my strategy was ridiculous.

"No, sir," I responded, at least confident I had given the correct answer.

"Then do what I taught you to do. Bring your breath to your center and allow your body to take over," he instructed.

I walked back to once again take a ready position, convinced that the suspension of my mind would certainly lead to my demise. A flurry of punches, kicks, and blocks ensued. Soon, I heard the sensei yell, "Finish him," indicating that one of us was on the floor. The standing opponent was to simply perform a short ritual of appreciation over the body of the fallen one. I had finished a kick by spinning in the opposite direction of my opponent, causing me to pause in order to figure out which one of us had fallen. Well, I was still standing, suggesting my challenger was down.

I performed the appropriate ritual with no idea how my opponent had found his way to the floor. Every time I tell this story, I am more convinced than ever that he must have tripped, possibly over his own feet. However, I did learn about the power of surrendering to the knowing of bodily instincts, and I was thankful for a body neither bloodied nor bruised. As much as our human nature is about having a body, it is also about having a mind, a mind that can support a mindful self-presence.

Mindful Self-Presence

> It is not sufficient just to have stability. It is necessary also to have clarity. That which prevents clarity is laxity, and what causes laxity is an over-withdrawal, excessive declination, of the mind. First of all, the mind becomes lax; this can lead to lethargy in which, losing the object of observation, you have as if fallen into darkness. This can lead even to sleep. When this occurs, it is necessary to raise or heighten the mode of apprehension. As a technique for that, think of something that you like, something that makes you joyous, or go to a high place where there is a vast view. This technique causes the deflated mind to heighten in its mode of apprehension.
>
> —The Dalai Lama

It can be a daunting task to find the stamina and courage to continue looking at what dwells in us. It appears that the Dalai Lama rightfully instructs us to lean into clarity if the fulfilling life is to be an option.

This is especially true for seekers. Without clarity we run the risk of wandering aimlessly, reacting to whatever gets our attention. The task will inevitably be challenged by the ego, determined to present itself as an exceptional finished product. However, if we can avoid lethargy and minimize pride, we can reap a number of significant benefits from mindful self-presence:

- Understanding of who we are and where we come from
- Less reactionaryism
- An ability to make decisions that are more informed by our desires and values
- Understanding what we do and do not have control over
- A greater capacity to let go of what we do not have control over
- A greater capacity to live with integrity, making our actions compatible with our personal values
- A greater ability to distinguish the stories we create about other people from the reality of who they actually are

There are four conditions that help to deepen a mindful self-presence: getting grounded, being in the present, developing an observer of our interior landscape, and committing to self-compassion. Let's discuss each of these in detail.

Getting Grounded

A person who doesn't breathe deeply reduces the life of the body. If he doesn't move freely, he restricts the life of his body. If he doesn't feel fully, he narrows the life of his body. And if his self-expression is constricted, he limits the life of his body.

—Alexander Lowen

Our planet likely got its origin as the result of a star or sun exploding, and therefore we can say that we are star beings. However, we are star beings living on a planet whose core is iron. It behooves seekers to claim their home on this iron rock. In fact, not to be at home on this rock may translate into one's feeling as if one is in exceptional danger. Claiming our home here means getting our bodies grounded to this rock. That can only happen if we have a connected relationship with our bodies and then allow our bodies to be connected to the ground.

A significant difference between seekers (or pilgrims) and tourists is that tourists do not get significantly involved with their experience. Involvement for the seeker is mandatory. An old meaning of the word *involved* is "to take in or roll into." The tourist observes experience and takes photographs, while the seeker becomes the experience. Hence, it serves the seeker to be curious about what makes it safe enough to take in or to roll into an experience.

Safety happens for the seeker through his or her getting grounded. Getting grounded offers a rootedness and solidity, and it reflects a conscious relationship to the earth beneath our feet. The safety offered by getting grounded is a measure of the relationship our bodies have with the ground at any given moment. To say we are rooted suggests that the forces of external winds cannot easily knock us down. People's opinions and attempts at influence over us do not easily sway and move us away from what is dear to us.

To be rootless is to be unsettled and wavering. Rootlessness makes it difficult to declare, "Here I am, in this place now, with this body, with these feelings, with this desire, and with these values." Of course, like any strength, being rooted can be pushed to extreme, where we become rigid in our beliefs and actions. Remaining close to the water of life, tears of sorrow and grief will likely prevent us from being rooted in dry, crusty earth.

The solidness provided by getting grounded offers a similar safety. When we are solid, we are not hollow and empty. Our presence with ourselves and our presence with others offer a substantial expression of our evolving uniqueness. Our attitudes and intentions possess a quality of being our own.

Yet rootedness and solidity do not guarantee we will not wander away from ourselves. Recently, a young man in the men's group I lead spoke about his considerable remorse regarding the choice to be deceitful in order to gain the favor of an attractive woman. He was grounded enough to realize he had wandered away from himself, and he also had a hunch about how to become more grounded. He started by simply telling the story of his loss of solidity, and then he reclaimed his rootedness by forgiving himself for not being honest. Those listening to the young man's story were keenly aware of the ground he typically lives on, reflected by the remorse he created for himself by stepping away from his personal values.

One of the listeners reminded him that even the most grounded among us will at one time or another lose rootedness. The man went on to recall that only Odysseus was clever enough to devise a plan to penetrate the walls of Troy. Yet on his way home from his victory at Troy, he was prepared to experience defeat by having sex with Circe and being turned into a pig as the outcome.

The young man continued to bring more meaning to his loss of groundedness as he asked: "What called me away from myself? What did I hope to gain by deceitfully calling the young woman to me?" With some support, he got to the understanding that he was attached to the young woman's confirming his beauty and his being lovable. He began to understand that becoming more grounded would require him to affirm his own beauty and the fact that he is lovable.

It might be helpful to list some strategies for getting grounded:

- Get serious about learning how to become more grounded.
- Bring more attention to your external sensory experience, meaning your vision, touch, hearing, taste, and sense of smell.

- Bring more attention to inner sensory experience—for example, awareness of breath; areas of energy tones such as tension and relaxation; and temperature, vitality, and fatigue.
- Bring more attention to the body's need for rest and movement.
- Ingest foods that neither arouse nor depress energy.
- Interrupt acting and speaking with excessive speed.
- Be aware of physical contact with the ground.
- Continue to return to the present by following the breath.
- Soften the jaw [my favorite].

Being in the Present

Because seekers are by definition visionaries, it is easy for them to get focused on and stuck in the future. That is not to say that only seekers have an extraordinary propensity for leaving the here and now: departure from the present is extremely popular. Popular psychology often suggests it just makes good sense to stay in the present, since that is where authentic empowerment takes place. That is certainly a worthwhile consideration because the present is where we can manifest our desires and allow our intentions to live. However, as much as it is a really good idea to return to the present, why we avoid going there may be a larger story.

Without a doubt, our access to authentic personal power happens in the moment. Nevertheless, the here and now is also where we are most vulnerable to getting hurt in a number of different ways. We can experience feeling forgotten, ridiculed, rejected, and shamed in the moment. As children, we figured out that to a great degree, feeling safe meant not being in the present—so we cleverly learned to maneuver out of the moment.

The dilemma is that the ingenuity that escorts us out of the present also nudges us away from ourselves, since self-presence happens in the moment. As Jack Kornfield (1993) says, "When we get caught up in the busyness of the world, we lose connection with one another—and ourselves." Speed is one of the most popular ways to leave the here and now. It keeps us rushing into the next moment; we maintain protection by being a moving target.

If our feelings were shamed during childhood, and if we slow down in the present, then we run the risk of feeling those feelings of shame, accompanied by our eroding self-worth. That constitutes a lot of feeling! When we wall off these feelings with increased life velocity, we diminish our capacity to be present. If we can allow ourselves to learn to feel the feelings and release the shame, we can begin to make peace with living in the moment. Or as Lowen points out, if we feel the feelings, we broaden the life of the body.

Learning to pause and breathe fully is a significant way to remain in and return to the moment. The pause becomes a welcome offered to what lives in us; fear, anger, sadness, and feeling lost and helpless may be some of what awaits us. Safety now translates into the welcome we offer these different feelings, coupled with compassion and acceptance.

Frank, a young psychologist, had been working with me for some time when he came to a session visibly upset. I allowed an initial silence to hang in the air, in the hope he might fill it with what distressed him.

"I want to kill that goddamn guy!" Frank exclaimed, willing to bring his disdain to the moment.

"Tell me what's got you so riled up," I invited.

"Well, a couple of years ago, I was working with a young man named Brad—a hard-core addict. I recommended that he attend residential treatment. Then his father came in and condemned me for not caring for his son, and then he ran out of my office!"

"I can imagine how misunderstood you felt. What became of Brad?"

"He left therapy, and a year and a half later he did enter residential treatment. I really hate his father, although I know I should forgive him. The father called me the other day and wants to come in and talk with me," Frank explained, his disgust palpable.

"Let me encourage you to put the intention to forgive the father on the back burner for now," I added.

"I feel vindictive. I'm not sure what to do with all these negative feelings," added Frank.

"Feel them and tell me what really gets you to want to retaliate," I suggested.

"Well, I guess the father really hurt me. I had been working with his son for several years. I really felt devoted to him and believed that without a significant intervention like residential treatment, his alcoholism would likely take a heavy toll on his life."

Frank spent a couple of sessions vacillating from acknowledging his hurt to wanting to attack Brad's father. It was obvious that Frank was struggling to welcome more inner toxic energy than he was accustomed to.

Several weeks later he met with Brad's father, who was deeply thankful for his son's newfound sobriety and very apologetic for having unjustly accused Frank of not treating his son appropriately. Frank was able to let go of his attachment to revenge and forgive Brad's father. Frank and I later spoke of how he had dropped into the present with pernicious feelings he was not accustomed to feeling and talking about. His permission to be present with these darker feelings allowed him to then be in the moment with the vulnerable truth of his hurt. Once he did that, his obsession with being vindictive greatly subsided.

Developing an Observer of Our Interior Landscape

If we are grounded and in the present, there will likely be much to observe that dwells within us. Hence, it empowers our self-presence to develop an observer, an act of mindfulness allowing us to give witness to our bodily sensations, our thoughts, and our emotions.

Without an observer, self-presence suffers two significant losses. The first loss is choice. With little or no observer, we react to our surroundings more. Someone says or does something and we respond automatically. Our freedom experiences a severe blow, limiting us to a single action. The observer separates us from what we are thinking and feeling, affording us the opportunity to consider alternative actions.

The second benefit of the observer is increased awareness of who we are. We can now devote ourselves to a self-examined life. Such a life enables us to develop inner authority, thus becoming more of an author of who we are. We create ourselves out of what we love, what we value, and what we believe.

The first object of observation can be our body, as we observe our external and internal sensations. We might notice that our breathing feels constricted in the presence of a certain person. If we are willing to extend credibility to the body's instinctual knowing, we can at least become receptive to the idea that more information will likely be revealed. Of course, this can be challenging, as the ego prefers to come up with some interesting idea rather than pay attention to what is going on in our bodies. Per a quote from Ernest Becker we first saw in Chapter 2, our bodies may remind us of our animal nature, which we would prefer to deny: "Man wants above all to endure and prosper, to achieve immortality in some way. Because he knows he is mortal, the thing he wants to do is to deny this mortality. Mortality is connected to the natural, animal side of his existence; and so man reaches beyond and away from that side."

If we can find the humility to reach back to our animal side, then we may allow ourselves to be informed by our bodies. We can open to some basic curiosities regarding our physical cues by asking these questions: Is my body reminding me of some emotional state I missed or ignored? If our bodies are responding in the presence of another person, then we can ask: How do I emotionally feel in this person's presence? Is there something I do not want to know about this person and me? Does this person remind me of anyone? Do I want something from this person? Do I carry some caution regarding this person?

Observing how our thoughts work is a second way to deepen our self-presence, especially if we do the witnessing without a load of criticism. We live in story: stories about ourselves, others, and God. If we do not know what story we are currently living in, we run the risk of acting from the story as if the story were an accurate account of reality.

Because the ego is strongly committed to protecting and proving, many of our stories are fueled by a need either to defend ourselves or to demonstrate something sterling about ourselves. Only a devoted practice of observing will increase our ability to know how much protection we actually need in any situation. The use of black-and-white language usually denotes we are in an inflated story not representative of reality. Saying words and phrases like "always," "never," "everyone," "no one," and "either this or that"—rather than "both this *and* that"—often suggest we are carrying a story not indicative of what's real.

An effective way of avoiding aggrandized stories about ourselves is to commit to feeling and observing how self-loathing lives in us. If we do not observe our self-ridicule, we run the risk of compensating for self-contempt by creating inflated stories about our competencies and contributions.

A third area of focus for the observer is our emotional life, which can be challenging to observe for several reasons:

- We continue to carry the internalized shame of having our emotions shamed by our parents.
- In order to avoid being shamed, we begin to repress or wall off our emotions, convinced they simply do not exist.
- If we received no support as a child when feeling the vulnerability associated with being frightened and hurt, it is

easy for us to believe that current support is not forthcoming, making it too dangerous to feel.

- We must deal with cultural injunctions that suggest a sobbing male is less than a real man and an angry female is a bitch.

However, there are also numerous benefits to observing our emotional lives:

- Our uniqueness lives in what we fear, how we hurt, what we find joyous, what makes us angry, and what we love.
- We run less of a risk of depressing emotional energy and becoming depressed.
- We experience less of a risk of experiencing a conversion reaction, in which emotional energy takes up residency in a physical symptom.
- We get to understand how we were emotionally injured along the way and what it means to bring healing to the injury.
- We do not automatically act out our emotions in a way that makes us risk harming others and/or ourselves.
- We get to name and express emotions, allowing us to interrupt emotional isolation where our uniqueness remains anonymous.
- With a greater ability to communicate emotions, we have a stronger capacity to build rapport and deepen trust with others.
- What we love becomes more available to us, offering us the ability to live our love.

Mindfulness practice means that we commit fully in each moment to be present; inviting ourselves to interface with this moment in full awareness, with the intention to embody the best we can an orientation of calmness, mindfulness, and equanimity right here and right now.
—Jon Kabat-Zinn

A wonderful strategy for developing an observer is the practice of *breath meditation*. While sitting comfortably with eyes closed, focused on the breath, we observe the stories entering the mind, interrupting the focus on breath. We then let go of the story and return to focus on the breath. The practice helps to limit the time we hang out in the myriad stories we are capable of creating. In order to find the resolve to continue to observe what lives in us, we will need to learn to hold what we observe with compassion.

Committing to Self-Compassion

Unfortunately, few of us experienced our childhood under watchful, gentle eyes and a compassionate voice. Authority figures often taught us to ridicule, shame, and reject what we observed about ourselves. The lack of kindness exhibited by our parents may have been sadistic, and in most cases, it was likely purposeful.

Our parents' toxic reactions to us had several purposes: to modify our behavior, to help our parents regain control over us, and to help them feel good about their parenting. As a result, our observations of ourselves lack compassion as we attempt to change our behavior, get back in control, and feel successful or simply good about ourselves. We can begin welcoming more compassion as we accept that a lack of kindness will not fulfill the above purposes. In fact, a lack of warmheartedness will probably inhibit mindfulness and separate us from ourselves. Why continue observing when it only leads to our feeling badly about ourselves?

Holding compassion for ourselves is analogous to encountering a good friend whose welcome and acceptance is easy to anticipate. The more we offer ourselves a greeting with kindness, the more eager we are to remain held in a mindful self-presence. The greatest challenge may be to remain mindful and compassionate while relating to others.

Self-Absence

We leave ourselves in a number of different ways, typically in the hope that life will be somehow more manageable if we do. Of course the opposite is true. It is critical for seekers to know when they have left themselves. We must be connected to the one doing the seeking in order to seek. It is analogous to separating from the leader of an expedition, in which case we run a high likelihood of wandering aimlessly. It is important to see self-absence as inevitable, with the evolving competency of knowing when we are separated from ourselves and what it will take to get back.

There are a number of ways we can become self-absent:

- *Loss of groundedness*—the more we lose connection to the ground, the further we travel away from ourselves.
- *Abuse of substances*—alcohol, pharmaceuticals, street drugs.
- *Depression*—diminished energy to the point that we cannot feel who we are or take the appropriate action to express who we are.
- *Hyperactivity*—amplified energy to the point that we are constantly leaning out of the present into the future.
- *Attachment to self-loathing*—defining us as incapable of taking the necessary risks to be the author of our lives.
- *Focus on innocuous details*—enabling us to be distracted by the task of generating meaning and depth, or as Kierkegaard described it, "tranquilized by trivia."

Mindful Self-Presence and Others

Jean Paul Sartre referred to being in the presence of others as "hell." His unfavorable description of social interaction captures the challenge of remaining true to ourselves while engaging others. The very presence of another person changes us. Our identities shift from being within ourselves to being witnessed and impacted by the choices of others.

I recently asked some extroverted friends if they defined social interaction as primarily about doing something with others, which they quickly confirmed. I pointed out that I had a different definition of social engagement, which raised some immediate curiosity. I explained that my description prioritized being with myself in the presence of others. To my surprise, they expressed sincere interest in exploring my account of social interaction. They went on to explain that their interest had to do with the numerous times they had left some social exchange feeling dissatisfied and unfulfilled. They realized how focused they had been upon what was being said by the other, responding so quickly that their mindful self-presence had been curtailed. How they felt and what they wanted often got lost in the exchange.

Besides simply getting lost in the conversation, we can also have our mindful self-presence undermined by several factors during social interaction:

- A need for approval
- A need to be impressive
- A need to compete
- A need to be included

The first step to gaining mindful self-presence during social interaction is to begin to devotionally develop an observer of one or more of the above needs while in conversation. Lively exchanges, although more exciting, tend to obstruct an awareness of these needs as they sit just below the surface. The key is to honor the value of pausing. It's possible for pausing, breathing, and noticing a need to impress to accompany an animated conversation. While in the presence of someone I trust, I find it helpful to say, "I'm aware I'm experiencing a need to impress you." The more compassion we can muster for this kind of mindfulness, the more we can make peace with our imperfect humanity.

The presence of others inevitably creates a degree of internal tension. We want to be seen, heard, appreciated, and loved. The issue is, will these desires drive us into seeking approval and therefore tug us away from ourselves? My hunch is that the answer is yes. If we focus on pausing and breathing, we can interrupt the magical thinking that we can ultimately control whether or not others will accept us. We can then return to what is in our control, namely how we receive ourselves.

As we gain more ability to mindfully return to ourselves, we can begin to allow our imaginations to illuminate possibilities. The more at home we are with ourselves, the more we might be willing to wander in non-conventional ways, less self-conscious about the uniqueness of our wanderings.

A Blessing for Presence

You seekers, the gods have ordained an arduous soul task for you. You are asked to remain students of presence, learning to endure the tension of a threshold dweller. May your endurance birth a deeper acceptance of what is and vision of what might be.

Do not be fooled by the quiet and stillness of your contracted presence. Its power remains delicate and muted, and yet it finds its way to the soul of one who suffers. For suffering knows and welcomes the softness of this presence.

A contracted presence asks for a humility, allowing you to step away from a display of skill and well-honed talent. The breath is your guide. The life you inhale toward the chambers of your heart brings a reassurance that life befriends the one who is vulnerable, the one who is lost, and the one who is alone.

You are asked to see your task more clearly, when there is a need for an expanded presence. That time requests a boldness, maybe to stand or to have a voice. Maybe even to simply move to the front of the bus. This may be a time of service, a gift to yourself or another. This offering may be a summons to move from ignorance to new eyes, from weakness to strength, or from disdain to compassion.

May you come to welcome your instinctual self-presence, sewed by the threads connecting you to all four-legged creatures. The knowledge of the cheetah, the elephant, and the wolf flowing through your bones as a primordial ooze. Become intimate with this energy as you run, dance, sing, and play. This presence is about being yourself and not about knowing yourself.

Your evolving humanity requests a mindful self-presence calling for your watchful eye. As you claim residency on this iron rock called Earth, you shall become more adept at seeing who you are. Full permission to your sensory experience will help make this rock your home. Smell the rock, see it, touch it, hear it, and eat what grows from it.

Your searching and visioning greatly depend upon how intimate you are with the moment. Only in being right here, right now, can you meet the soul's essential need to give and receive. The moment is where love lives. Feed it well, for it is pregnant with your future.

In this now, you may observe some small expression of the one you call "I." You can witness different physical and emotional tones that contribute to the opus of the self. And then notice the endless stories created by you, the maker of meaning. And now a more demanding task, letting stories of incrimination fade, making room for the light of compassion.

And then only another strenuous task, to remember to notice yourself in the presence of another. Involved, yet detached enough to see and possibly relinquish ties to impressing, saving, competing, and seeking approval. All of which inhibit the emergence of something deeper within you, as well as seeing some assistance offered by life in support of your quest.

4

Imagination

The awakened imagination desists from this domestication. It returns us to our native wildness, to the natural and seamless fluency of our own nature. Other worlds come into view and we are invited to risk new and original ways of dwelling in the world.

—John O'Donohue

THE ABOVE QUOTE SUGGESTS THAT as we move closer to our true natures, we may find the courage to see with new eyes, risking to live in unique ways that reflect the deepest part of ourselves. An old definition of the word *imagination* is "naturally suited to." It may be that the first thing to imagine is possessing eyes naturally suited to seeing a unique and evolving internal landscape.

Seekers are midwives, helping some vision of home to be born from the way we hold our injuries, sorrows, joys, and passions. The emergence of imagination happens as we refuse to live at a distance from ourselves. That refusal demands to know where we belong. And at the threshold, we hold the curiosity that eagerly seeks home. We now can imagine what might be calling to our true natures.

I received early lessons about imagination from the Scots-Irish men in my family. My body housed the lessons from the stories they told, and many years later, I would begin to decipher my visceral knowing. They hungered to know where love lived and welcomed the journey into the mystery of love, not taking comfort in some provincial knowing. Their gods were curiosity, wonder, and novelty. As they inseminated their lives with these energies, they gave birth to creativity. They held an abiding faith in the sacred ordinary and remained suspicious of anything calling them away from simplicity.

In this chapter I'll share some of my early lessons about imagination and also explore how family and culture shape imagination; the four energies of imagination—curiosity, wonder, novelty, and creativity; Eros, friend of imagination; and why the *sacred ordinary* is critical to the seeker's developing greater imagination.

The Early Lessons

A father, grandfather, and uncles who were Celtic storytellers blessed me early in my childhood with a flair for living in stories that fed their wildness. The most vivid memories of my childhood include Sunday visits to my grandparents' house, where the women gathered in the kitchen and the men assembled in the living room. Until I was five, I was more or less restricted to the kitchen. Then shortly after my fifth birthday, my grandmother escorted me to the living room, proudly presenting me to the men.

"My grandson has come to school age and he'll be joining you. I expect you'll be watching your manly ways. Teach him well and above all, don't be taking the Lord's name in vain while he sits with you," instructed my grandmother, with an apparent hope that these Scots-Irish rogues would honor her request.

"Certainly, ma'am, yes, ma'am. We'll be watching over the lad with the hand of Michael the Archangel himself," responded her five sons, three sons-in-law, and a husband who raised his glass of ale as if offering a toast to his wife's appeal.

"That son of a bitch Father Sullivan has got some goddamn nerve entertaining the widow Mary O'Leary," yelled my Uncle Tom as my grandmother closed the door separating the kitchen from the living room, her urging disappearing behind cigar smoke and the smell of brew.

"I don't know. I think the priest has been very helpful to Mary since Jack's death," reported my Uncle Joe, with a cautious drop in intonation.

"Helpful! She's not just bringing the priest warm muffins! He's got her blowing a tune on Gabriel's horn!" declared my Uncle Luke, relinquishing the timidity normally indicative of a son-in-law who was relatively new to this gathering.

"He may have made that popular promise, you know: play the right tune on the horn and the pearly gates swing wide open," added my Uncle Jake, receiving an even more robust response from the group.

"The priest helped the Malinski family when their boy was killed by a drunk driver," suggested my Uncle Patrick, bringing a momentary stillness to the assembly.

"Maybe that was his way of keeping the Polacks in the parish from questioning any favoritism he might show to his own kind," suggested my Uncle Tom, glancing over toward Peter, the Polish son-in-law.

"I like the priest. Maybe if your old ladies were baking some of those muffins and playing the extended version of 'Hark, The Herald Angels' on your horn, we might extend some consideration to the old priest," added my Uncle Bill, exhibiting an unusual boldness for a son-in-law seeking the favor of this gathering.

"I don't want to mock Jack's passing by bringing shit to Mary's relationship with Father Sullivan," voiced my Uncle Jake, arousing more of the group's agreement.

"Father Sullivan might be getting his, and he might be bringing some comfort to Jack's wife," added my grandfather, bringing a deep calm to the room.

I recall my Uncle Tom then telling a story that made each man curl over in hilarity. When the laughter subsided, one of the sons-in-law asked, "Did that really happen?"

He was new to the gathering and had no way of knowing that that question had no place in this room. It bordered on blasphemy, an insult to the culture that gathered here. The question reflected how much he did not understand these men. Atypical of the norm, no one responded to him. It was as if they all knew that the question reflected how much of a foreigner the new son-in-law was to the culture. What it would take to integrate him was not going to take place over the next few minutes. It would only be years later that I came to understand the nature of the sacredness violated by the question, did that really happen?

These men did not simply tell stories. They lived in story. There were two realities for them: the seen and the unseen. They lived a seamless connection from one dimension to the other. Although burdened by an intimate connection to alcohol, their spirits were naturally suited to live in story.

Living in story is about fire. These men lived with a flame that burned away an attachment to convention and social expectation. The inner blaze cleared the brush of propriety and in doing so made space for their creative energies. They replaced the seen with the unseen of their longings, their wit, their love, and their passion. The seen, or the external world, existed as a place to bring voice to their stories and allow their stories to be infused with new meanings.

They ruthlessly disallowed the roles they played to extinguish the fire. Their Sunday gatherings served as a place to rekindle the fire, reminding one another who they were and the stories they lived in. I later would discover that the furnace needed to hold their fire might have been a bit small. Without the necessary grounding of their fire, many of their gifts would have gone unlived. My challenge was to see what they gave me directly and what was lost in their lives, so that I might learn to augment the legacy of loss. Some of these augmented lessons are as follows:

- Do what is naturally suited to you.
- Identify what attachments to convention need interruption in order to live what is naturally suited to you.
- Ask yourself, what scares me about interrupting my attachment to this aspect of convention?
- Ask yourself, how do I carry this fear creatively?
- Allow what is naturally suited to you to create the story you are destined to live in.
- Ground your fire, allowing its warmth to guide the development and manifestation of your gifts. This means employing the kind of boundaries that prevent passion or fire from destroying what you hold dear, especially living your gifts.
- Deepen your story by asking yourself, what do I ask of this story, and what does this story ask of me?
- Travel with those who support and honor the story you live in.
- Let the above questions point you toward what you seek, especially pertaining to love.

Imagining Where Love Lives

Seekers are asked to take on the task of loving life, demanding arduous imaging into where love might live. Our experiences of love are vast, sometimes magical and enchanting, sometimes filled with sorrow and heartbreak. We imagine into love so we might know where to stand, where to open our heart to both love's sweetness and love's challenges. Our love instructions come from early family and from cultural influences. I want to share my own early lessons regarding love and how they impact my seeking of love today.

Family Images

Several astrological readings I have received suggest that what is naturally suited to me is being a husband. When I first heard such an account of my identity, I quietly wept in honor of an understanding I had kept secret, even to myself. After the ending of a twenty-five-year marriage, I dated a woman for seven years. I decided to marry again. I was scared that I would not do it right a second time, which reflected my attachment to the conventional perspective that a successful marriage is reflected by longevity. If I were to let go of my attachment, then I would need to create my own criteria for a successful marriage.

Five months into my second marriage, I declared the need for a separation and likely a divorce. I feared that I had made a mistake, and I was also scared someone would discover the foolishness of my ways. My wife asked if I would be willing to find a marriage counselor and explore how I got to my need for separation. I agreed; it suited me to get help for such a large life decision.

The counseling session began with the counselor wanting to focus on my discontent. After rambling a bit, he asked, "So tell me how you've come to decide to leave this marriage."

I took several deep breaths, and the words that came out of my mouth seemed to speak of their own accord, without any intention of mine. "There's no pain here," I uttered repeatedly, tears pouring down my cheeks.

The counselor turned to my spouse and asked, "Can you hear what he's saying?"

She nodded in the affirmative, and I continued to sob, bewildered by how the absence of pain could be a good reason to leave someone. By the end of the session, I was questioning what this story was asking of me. I came to realize that most of my life I had associated love with pain and deprivation. How could there be love with no pain? The story was likely asking me to explore receiving love that was mostly pain-free. I wanted to learn about love.

Where did the love story laced with pain and deprivation come from? I knew I needed to imagine how a love story so strongly driven by deprivation came to live in my soul—so strongly that I was willing to let go of love that did not deprive.

Images of my early family experience began beckoning me. One Christmas Eve when I was in my early thirties, I sat enjoying a glass of yuletide eggnog with my parents. I looked toward my mother and proceeded to thank her for the fond memories I had of her affection and warmth.

A dense silence ensued, interrupted by my mother saying, "I had trouble having physical contact with you. But your father was very affectionate."

I attempted to interrupt my tendency to get distracted by my mother's emotional detachment and instead experience her candor as loving. I then spent weeks attempting to make sense of my maternal memories. Could I have made up all these fond recollections? Was I crazy? Or had I simply taken care of myself in the midst of some significant emotional impoverishment? I realized that I needed to accept how I had taken care of myself and to allow my attachment to deprivation to show me how I wanted love to live in my life now.

My attachment to idealizing love became increasingly obvious. The idealization of the "house of love" had become my guarantee of generating deprivation, since flawless love was not a real-life option. So, although I knew very little about love not grounded in deprivation and idealization, I held an image of myself as a man willing to develop the capacity to receive such love. I also saw the gifts I brought to my marriage, such as the willingness to be honest, accountable for my behavior, and encouraging to my spouse, as well as the ability to request what I wanted from her while holding myself primarily responsible for my happiness.

The story continues to ask me to be a student of love and emotional intimacy. I bring my curiosity to the task, noticing that my spouse inevitably calls me to some place I've never been before. Of late, the new territory has been to drop into feelings of vulnerability rather than attempting to dominate or influence her in some way. The story also has asked me to get honest about my attraction to deprivation. I can easily be aroused and drawn to it.

I've come to accept that I will likely never completely eliminate being pulled in the direction of emotional deprivation, the place where I am not seen, heard, understood, and supported. To some degree, this lure reflects my soul's deep loyalty to where I came from as a child. I simply seek to be he who gives love and receives love with those who are also willing to take on the challenges of loving.

Cultural Images

Cultural images of where love lives vary from the excessively romantic, lacking the resolve and suppleness needed to sustain a life of heart, to a more cynical path, paved with unbridled defenses against hurt and vulnerability. The longing of the maturing heart is for love neither smothered by excessive sentiment nor starved by the barrenness of unrestrained detachment. Our challenge is to move away from a satisfaction in our search that finds solace in mediocrity. We are called to look toward cultural images of love again and again, with new eyes.

One set of images will assuredly come from the Judeo-Christian creation myth, the story of Adam and Eve. Most of us are familiar with the religious perspective of the narrative, which suggests Eve (the daughter) is unloving as she disobeys God (the father). She is then punished, banished from the Garden along with Adam. We can imagine into this story with a new set of images, bringing new and deeper insights about parenting and love.

We first notice that there is no mention of a mother in the story, which was likely written around 600 BCE. Might the absence of a mother reflect the strength of the patriarchy at that time? Does it suggest that most of us will be overtly loved and guided in childhood by one parent? Could it be that the love of the second parent will likely be more subtle and muted? Are we asked to reflect more deeply on the love of the secondary parent, rather than simply writing his or her offerings off as nonexistent or ineffectual? And can we see how love actually lived with this secondary parent, not settling for defining ourselves as simply forgotten?

The father in our creation myth declares, "The tree of knowledge of good and evil you must not eat; for the day you eat of it, you must die." Thus we are initially offered foreshadowing of an impending death. Then there is reference to the innocence of Adam and Eve— "Naked with no shame."

We can imagine knowledge of good and evil marking the end of innocence, with the mandate "you must die" reflecting the death of childhood. Images also surface regarding the father being attached to keeping his offspring childlike, with some resistance to their moving into adulthood. Can we say that images of parental love often possess a theme of fostering dependency in children? Does such dependence allow the parent to remain a parent, needed and respected? Does such love suggest that children will need to steal their autonomy and evolving adulthood? Will the support of a child's growth and maturation have to come from the child and not the parent?

The serpent in the story declares, "If you eat it, your eyes will be opened and you will be like God." Almost every culture, including India and the native peoples of North and South America, viewed the serpent as a symbol of renewal, rebirth, and immortality. We might then see the serpent as tempting Eve to be reborn into her womanhood. This leaves Eve with the existential predicament of choosing to obey either her father or her soul's task.

Can we image the story informing us that our emotional and spiritual development will greatly depend upon how much love and devotion we bring to the path of our own souls? Are we called to be courageous enough to face possible rejection and dismissal by some authority figure? This dilemma can be lived out in the context of a parent, spouse, friend, or boss.

The story ends with God instructing an angel to guard the tree of life, which yields immortality. Again, are we being reminded that a parent's love may not encourage the child to be as knowledgeable or as strong as the parent? We can wonder if it is even possible to love and be loved if we don't leave the Garden, remaining loyal and obedient to the parent's values. We cannot borrow what someone else cherishes and hope to be loved for who we are.

When we leave the Garden, we claim our uniqueness, reflected in our own values and beliefs. Now we can be loved for who we are. There may be images in our creation myth suggesting that betraying the parent and risking banishment are likely prerequisites for entering the house of love. And can we imagine that love and betrayal are inextricably connected? In a committed relationship, could it be that we either betray the other, are betrayed by the other, or betray ourselves? It will take some powerful energies vitalizing our imagining to hold images like betrayal and love in a dialectical relationship that works.

The Four Energies of Imagination

Four energies instill life in imagination. These forces include curiosity, wonder, novelty, and creativity. These energies also reflect the pulse of threshold dwellers. Let's look at each of these in detail.

Curiosity

Old meanings of the word *curious* include "eager to know" and "full of care." "Eager to know" sits easily with our contemporary understanding of the word. However, it is important to note that we typically favor knowing over being eager to know. That subtle shift can easily place us at odds with curiosity, which suggests that the state of knowing has not yet taken place. The challenge may be to dethrone knowing, replacing it with an eagerness to know.

Taking up the cause of *curiosity* means taking on the task of letting go of the culture's condemnation of confusion and its adoration of knowing. Confusion is often explained as the result of being intellectually flawed. We either go into denial of our confusion or inhibit any voice revealing its presence. The irony is that confusion or unknowing is what typically gives rise to curiosity. It can be a helpful practice to de-shame confusion. Shame insidiously accompanies confusion when we decide we don't know and others do know. It can be helpful to shift out of the story, "I'm the only one who is confused and therefore intellectually lacking" to "I'm confused about this particular topic because my attention has been elsewhere, and this is not a commentary about my intellectual ability."

Favorable social reactions are common to those claiming to know. To be in the know suggests that I am somehow a valuable resource— needed, possibly admired—and that my knowledge base may even be some kind of declaration of manhood. It is somewhat countercultural to claim being mostly curious rather than knowledgeable. As a curious man, Albert Einstein found himself confused by his countercultural self-definition: "I don't understand why I am receiving so many job offers. I am only extremely curious."

It may be helpful to look at the second definition of the word *curious*: "full of care." What is being suggested here is that curiosity keeps us in relationship to mystery. Our care is expressed by honoring the immensity of the unknown, continuing to receive more from the endless mystery of life. The questions, *What else is here?* and *What remains hidden?* bring the fullness of care to our eagerness.

The men in my grandmother's living room brought great care to their eagerness to know. Whether they were assessing a particular political position or evaluating the moral character of a member of the clergy, they passionately and humorously built their individual and collective stories. Each image in the stories received distinct attention. Unparalleled scrutiny inevitably weighed in until themes of the sacred and the profane received their just due. These men were intolerant of an image receiving excessive righteousness and almost as intolerant of the impious acquiring too much consideration.

There was nothing about their eagerness to know that was pristine. Their curiosity was driven by passion, competition, humor, and a desire to be blessed by my grandfather. They filled their stories with care because it was where they lived. The care had little to do with drawing conclusions. It was much more about the delight of creating the story and loving one another through story.

Wonder

> So, when after having made every effort to understand, we are ready to take upon ourselves the mystery of things, then the most trivial of happenings is touched by wonder, and there may come to us, by grace, a moment of unclouded vision.
>
> —Helen Luke

Curiosity is the eagerness and care driving an inquiry, while *wonder* is the admiration and awe we feel due to what curiosity reveals to us. The word *wonder* is connected to the word *wonderful*, which translates to "full of wonder."

The men in my childhood saw their life experience as demanding a full response. They responded to fear, disappointment, and loss with enough enthusiasm and humor to honor the absurdity of their actions. Their stories included a strong theme of anticipation that life would offer them an opportunity to respond with a full heart, either in applause or condemnation. Neutrality was not an option. Such anticipation bonded them to their lived experience in a revelry accompanied by awe. There was a betrothal to the moment, what it would give them and what they would give back to it in story.

We don't generate wonder—it comes to us. It is received as we loosen our grip on being well positioned with cherished beliefs, opinions, and values. Children are well disposed to wonder because their innocence exists in lieu of being well positioned. Their senses and minds are perched, prepared to be aroused by life's offerings. This does not mean that we are supposed to become children and somehow not be well positioned; our maturation and character depend upon us taking on a personal worldview, one we can truly call our own.

The key is not to succumb to the ego, which attempts to assert its sovereignty by deciding that it is familiar with every life encounter. Nothing is truly new to a zealous ego dedicated to demonstrating its alleged boundless knowledge. But how do we deepen our receptivity to wonder once we have established a well-developed belief system? We can notice the meanings we are ready to attribute to our experience and then ask, "What else is here?"

Wonder asks us to renew our relationship to mystery. Not the relationship of a child, based upon innocence, but rather a relationship that embraces the largeness of the unknown, the immensity of our potential experience. If we can muster enough humility to accept the limits of the beliefs we have groomed over time, then we can honor what life has taught us while remaining a student of life's enormity.

Novelty

> *All this was new to me. Life takes us by surprise and orders us to move towards the unknown—even when we don't want to and we think we don't need to.*
> —Paulo Coelho

Seeing newness depends upon what we see as much as what we bring to the eyes doing the seeing. Novelty is sacrificed when the vibrancy of our feeling, instincts, and intuitions flatline and we then see through a fog of repetition.

Opening to wonder and novelty greatly depends upon our relationship to surprise. We might resist being surprised for a number of reasons. Surprise presents a serious insult to the ego's attachment to being in control. Surprise suggests we are on an extremely unpredictable journey, with change as the only constant. We are not taught how to make peace with such an adventure. We fall back upon disbelief again and again, refusing to accept the perilous nature of the journey. When surprise insinuates some expression of our mortality, fictitious expressions of security begin to quake. Bank accounts, prestige, political influence, and various achievements become anemic, unable to protect us from the fragility accompanying our mortality.

There is also the misguided perception that living from surprise is indicative of childhood. Real adults have seen and experienced it all. This ego-driven thinking places adults in an alleged mastery of life, rather than letting them be guided by the curiosity and wonder reflective of students devoted to life's mystery.

I was recently surprised to hear that a dear old friend was succumbing to advanced cancer. Although I knew he was being treated for the disease, my denial was jolted when the announcement came that he might not be with us at Thanksgiving. My vision of the longevity of our relationship was surprisingly and abruptly interrupted.

Another friend and I decided to visit our mutual friend in his last days. As we approached the home of our dying friend, I was surprised by a strong sense of inadequacy running through me. I was convinced that I was not going to be able to offer him what he needed. I had helped many folks in their process of accompanying the death of a loved one. However, I realized I had never personally accompanied someone in his dying.

Surprise typically asks for something, and this was no different. We entered the home surprised to see the man we had known as robust and muscular now hollow-cheeked and emaciated. I was being asked to let go of the typical hardy, energetic greeting I was accustomed to and being petitioned to drop into a more tender and gentle engagement, which itself announced the magnitude of my friend's condition.

Another demand of the surprise was the request to open my heart to my friend's fragility, letting go my attachment to some healthier version of him. And finally, the surprise was asking me to accept non-permanence and the vulnerability of my own mortality. The frail body before me, which resembled more a child than a man, sat in waiting in my own destiny.

"They told me I could fight this. I guess I lost the battle," uttered my friend, summoning enough breath to speak clearly, giving testimony to his alleged failure.

"Oh no, my friend! You have not lived life mostly as a warrior seeking victories! You lived as a lover! I know the generosity of attention and support you offered so many who were struggling with addiction," I declared passionately, more as a pronouncement of my love for his work than an attempt to convert him to my view.

"I just thought I might have had a chance to win this battle," he added.

"You and I have again and again protested the will of the gods. So many times we did not accept what the gods presented us. Ours was to learn to find some level of acceptance of all that was out of our control. You can pretend your will is greater that the decree of the gods or find that this too is out of your control and ask for acceptance," I suggested, aware I was speaking more to myself than to my friend.

"I can't control these goddamn tumors. That's the bottom line."

"No, you can't. You can ask for the grace to accept the cards Fate has dealt you."

"I can see that acceptance is once again my lesson. I also want to receive the love of the men who have walked with me," he admitted.

A week later, seven of Norbert's friends and his son gathered around him. The bedroom had been transformed into a hospital setting, with a glass with a straw, a plastic urinal, and various medications scattered about. A window was wide open, filling the room with crisp Vermont air, bringing Norbert as close as he could get to the outdoors. None of us wanted this to be a good-bye to our friend, and our resistance initially weighed on us.

We took turns telling Norbert how his life had benefited us. Some men paused, allowing their tears to take them to the next sentence. Each man in his own way blessed the largeness of Norbert's heart. We had moved into a celebration of our friend's heart—a heart that knew no pretense and took great joy in giving anonymously, almost viewing any acknowledgement of his many offerings as a prostitution of his giving. The generosity of his attention and support had touched my life many times, most vividly in the interruption of my attachment to alcohol.

I reminded Norbert of a regular ritual I performed. On a wall in my bedroom was a picture of my son and me. I would approach the picture weekly, gaze into the eyes of my son, and say, "It ends with me!" Norbert's commitment to my recovery had translated into a devotional interruption of a painful legacy.

None of us really knew how to leave our friend that day. On some level, we each pretended there might be another day—another time for stories, for laughter, and for growing a friendship. None of us were prepared for our loss, and waiting for each of us was the unpredictability and surprise of a life without our friend.

Remaining open and receptive to being surprised calls for a suppleness of spirit and a humility that embraces limits with a measure of grace. With these influences in place, we do not have to be bigger than life. We can be surprised, noticing that we are likely being called somewhere we have not been before. From such a call we can animate life, experiencing it as living us. This kind of relatedness—we live life and life lives us—is intimate. The beauty of such a connection is that the heart that lives there longs to create.

Creativity

> *Human freedom involves our capacity to pause between the stimulus and response and, in that pause, to choose the one response toward which we wish to throw our weight. . . . Clearly self-creating is actualized by our hopes, our ideals, our images, and all sorts of imagined constructs that we may hold from time to time in the forefront of our attention.*
>
> —Rollo May

Creativity and imagination form a deeply mutual relationship, one being fed by the other. Imagination can be seen as the muse for creativity and creativity as the concrete expression of imagination. It is only too easy to limit creativity to traditional art forms: writing, painting, sculpture, drawing, pottery, and photography. The opportunity to create or grow ourselves happens in each "pause," where imagination has the opportunity to arouse movement by presenting some image.

From the above quote we can glean at least three important considerations about creativity and its relationship to imagining: 1) being able to pause in the moment in order to notice what is asking for our attention, 2) bringing our intellectual and emotional "weight" to what is asking for our attention, and 3) seeing our creative task as creating ourselves. May goes on to say that it takes courage, opening to risks, fearing the unknown, and yet stepping somewhere revealing a new layer of self.

An example of pausing mindfully to decide where to bring the weight of our intellectual and emotional attention may be helpful.

In this story about my friend Steve, you can see how our imagining contributes to our creative expression and our creativity gives inspiration to our imagining. Steve is an old friend who has served for years in an organization committed to addressing environmental concerns. The following conversation between Steve and me reflects a challenge he faced that called him to deeper levels of imagination and creativity.

"There has been some conflict and upheaval in our organization regarding the role of leadership," explained Steve.

"What have been the main points of discussion?" I asked.

"Well, as you know, I have been offering leadership there for years. Burt, who has been involved in various leadership positions in our organization, suggested he and I exchange letters describing our different views about leadership."

"How did it go?"

"I may have been a bit naïve. I simply thought we were both dedicated to resolving any divisiveness that might be harmful to the organization," Steve recounted, his voice dropping off.

"It sounds like the e-mail exchanges went in a different direction."

"Yeah, Burt began to use the alleged forum for exploring leadership as a way to attack my character. I felt angry, hurt, and confused about how to proceed with him. I knew that whatever action I took would reverberate throughout the organization," Steve expressed, his tone and gestures depicting the weight of the challenge.

"What did you do next?" I asked.

"Well, I knew it would not be a good idea to respond abruptly. So I took some time to consider what was important for me and what it was I wanted to see happen," he explained.

"I appreciate the time you took to see what really mattered to you," I added.

"I knew I was committed to doing whatever I could to diminish and hopefully eliminate divisiveness in our organization. Because I felt personally offended, I was overwhelmed with the task I was facing.

I decided I did not want just to write Burt off, yet I didn't want to overlook the toxic feature of his communication with me either."

"Steve, I can't imagine how you handled all of this!"

"The last message I received from Burt moved me into action," Steve said. "It read, 'Any giving of time and energy you have offered the organization was simply your egotistical way of gaining attention and self-inflating.' I decided it was definitely time for us to meet in person."

"I really don't know how I would have approached this kind of dilemma," I shared.

"I also became aware of how silly it would be for me to offer reasons why the offerings I've made to the organization were done mostly in the best interest of the association. Of course, I was fantasizing that Burt might just walk in and say he regretted making those remarks. But that did not happen," explained Steve.

"God, I hope it went well for you."

"I arrived at the restaurant a few minutes before our scheduled time in order not to feel rushed. Burt arrived shortly thereafter and we exchanged a few pleasantries. I then turned the conversation to our letters. I suggested that there must be literally endless ways to interpret how a man leads and gives to an organization, which Burt readily agreed to. Then I added that there are at least 150 ways to see what I have done in our organization, to which Burt once again agreed. I then laid on the table a copy of the letter he had sent, the one charging me with excessive self-inflation. That generated an extended silence. I then asked Burt, 'How did you come to decide to choose interpretation number 125 as the way to see me?'"

"It must have been an uncomfortable moment for the both of you," I said.

"At that point my anxiety subsided. The air was heavy with the viscosity of Burt's disorientation. He sat motionless until a buildup of saliva forced a large gulp, followed by him saying 'I knew I would learn something from you today.'"

"Where did the conversation go from there?'"

"It didn't go much further. I did not want to contribute to the divisiveness. I had simply held up a mirror to which he could react any way he wished," Steve stated, with a gentle nod.

I went on to let Steve know how much I appreciated the beauty and grace reflected by his choice to engage Burt. Steve was faced with the challenge of holding his hurt and anger, not allowing it to dictate how he related to Burt. He knew that the conversation could have fallen into a series of charges and countercharges of poor character, contributing to greater divisiveness in the organization. I told Steve how much I respected the way he had imagined into the conversation with Burt (something we describe in the next section) and brought forward what needed to be said without betraying himself or attacking Burt.

Steve modeled for me what it means to honor what lives in us as a way to create who we are. The beauty in Steve's choice was an unfolding of truth and compassion. Something was preserved in Steve's actions. It might have been the dignity of both men and the honoring of an organization they both love. I was reminded that there lies in each of us some embryo waiting to be birthed. We are meant to birth over and over again, and this is our creative quest. We are asked to go down into the depths of our soul in order to invite what is stirring there, asking for life.

Eros: Friend of Imagination

> *Go into yourself. . . . Describe your sorrows and desires,*
> *the thoughts that pass through your mind and your belief*
> *in some kind of beauty—describe all these with heartfelt,*
> *silent, humble sincerity and, when you express yourself,*
> *use the Things around you, the images from your dreams,*
> *and the objects that you remember. If your everyday life*

seems poor, don't blame it; blame yourself; admit to
yourself that you are not enough of a poet to call forth
its riches; because for the creator there is not poverty and
no poor indifferent place. . . . Try to raise up the sunken
feelings of this enormous past; your personality will grow
stronger, your solitude will expand and become a place
where you can live in twilight, where the noise of other
people passes by, far in the distance.
                                            —Rainer Maria Rilke

Before Steve met with Burt, he allowed himself to call to mind images of the hollow victories and shameful defeats he had experienced with other men. He recalled the deep feelings of loss he went through when attempting to persuade someone that he was right. He recounted his fear of standing alone and how it had ignited a campaign to convert others to his way of thinking. He also remembered the estrangement resulting as folks distanced themselves from him in an attempt to avoid his recruitment. He felt a cold shiver in his body, created by his attachment to being right and how it had isolated him from himself and others. He went down into himself before his meeting with Burt.

It would have been only too easy for Steve to see his past as simply unfortunate. Yet by welcoming that past, his previous choices held a hidden power to create. It reminded me of an old mentor of mine, of whom I asked, "How did you become so mindful?"

"I made many mistakes," he replied, "leaving me with many teachers."

How can making mistakes be so essential to creativity? The obvious response is that mistakes instruct by exposing us to what doesn't work. However, just below the surface, the mistakes likely reflect the courage to risk. And the risks are likely expressions of some delicious seduction where Eros, the god of love, reigns. Each risk calls us to some intimate connection with life. Such an intimacy is likely to be consummated by some passionate insemination—the creative moment. Carl Jung describes this as follows:

Looking, psychologically, brings about the activation
of the object; it is as if something were emanating
from one's spiritual eye that evokes or activates the
object of one's vision. The English verb "to look
at" does not convey this meaning, but the German
betrachten, which is an equivalent, means also to make
pregnant . . . . And if it is pregnant, then something
is due to come out of it; it is alive, it produces, it
multiplies.

Jung is implying that a look "emanating from one's spiritual eye" has
the transformative power of Eros. We are impregnating an object or
an image of our observation with a myriad of possibilities, everything
from the sacred to the profane. When our gaze is instilled with the
passion of Eros, then our relationship to what is observed changes,
the object or image observed changes, and we change. For example,
if we see a place or a person with reverence, then it is likely that we
will treat that place or person with reverence.

We see this similar theme of creative intimacy in the Native
American tradition. As Chief Seattle said, "Humankind has not
woven the web of life. We are but one thread within it. Whatever
we do to the web, we do to ourselves. All things are bound together.
All things connect." Chief Seattle stresses that we create ourselves
as we treat the web of life. Scientists also remind us of the intimate
connection that we observers have to what we observe. This position
was first presented by the physicist Werner Heisenberg, who said,
"Separation of the observer from the phenomenon to be observed is
no longer possible."

These themes of intimate connection coming from psychological
perspectives, indigenous views, and the scientific community appear
to be proposing that the creative moment cannot be avoided. We
are creating by way of what we bring or don't bring to our attention.
Reverence, irreverence, or indifference drives how we see and act.

How we relate to what we are observing brings some new dimension to ourselves and to what we are observing.

An example of this co-creative process may be helpful. I recently heard of a preacher from the West Coast who wished to have a better understanding of those who are homeless. So he decided to take to the streets in daily search of food and shelter. He spent two weeks moving amongst the homeless as one of them. As a result, his view of the homeless was kindled with deep compassion and accompanied by a new understanding of the folks he traveled with. He saw the role of addiction and mental illness. He saw how one mistake could totally derail an entire life. He was changing, and the way he interacted with the homeless was changing. They were no longer simply a population unwilling to work and become financially solvent. And as his relationship to the homeless changed, could we assume that the homeless he encountered were also changing in his presence?

The homeless called him to a deeper place in himself, and he expressed a deeper curiosity about who he was before his homeless days. Carl Jung suggested, "At the bottom of the soul, you find humanity." Hence, the creative act always holds some potential for the sublime mingling of the individual with the universal. At any moment we can take Rilke's recommendation and go into ourselves, unearthing our longing, sorrow, and passion, which become energies of insemination. This process is not meant to be reserved for exceptional experiences, but rather for ordinary times and days.

The Sacred Ordinary

The invariable mark of wisdom is to see the miraculous in the common.

—Ralph Waldo Emerson

The most significant impediment for the seeker desiring to live with more imagination is to ignore what is ordinary and close by. As you read in the quote that began the previous section, the poet Rilke implores us to pay attention to our everyday life: "If your everyday life seems poor, don't blame it; blame yourself . . . that you are not enough of a poet to call forth its riches; because for the Creator there is not poverty and no poor indifferent place."

Darwin suggested that the purpose of human emotion is action. I would offer that the purpose of our imagination is also action. An old definition of the word *poet* is "to make or compose." Rilke challenges us to be moved toward making and composing because of our relationship with the richness of the ordinary, the sacred ordinary. What we make may be a new attitude or action, not limiting ourselves to generating something that astounds art critics.

One example of the sacred ordinary happened years ago while my twelve-year-old son, a friend, and I were visiting Weston Priory in Vermont. We were walking from the car toward the gift shop at the Priory when a monk harvesting potatoes caught my attention. I encouraged my friend and my son to continue making their way to the gift shop, but I did not understand why witnessing a man plucking potatoes from the soil mesmerized me. I knew I was not simply pausing to watch some agrarian act take place. I stood there for an extended time, unable to interrupt my gaze, which was locked on the ordinary task of collecting vegetables.

It would be years later when I learned that in the sixth century, St. Benedict called his monks to live with a loyalty to the present. I had witnessed a monk exhibiting his devotion to the present while harvesting potatoes. I had seen a living prayer, what I sometimes refer back to as the Potato Prayer. Never before had I viewed a simple task being draped with grace, infusing the ordinary with the sacred.

The sacred ordinary revealed itself once again after a weekend retreat with Matthew Fox. During the weekend, Fox referenced the power of being able to be grateful for a single breath. I knew immediately that I had never been thankful for a lot of breaths, never mind a single one. The challenge and invitation to be able to experience that kind of gratitude intrigued me. I left the weekend hoping that someday, I might know that level of appreciation.

The next day around noon, I took several sips of lemonade and immediately experienced a spasming esophagus. Unable to get a breath, I made futile attempts to bang on my back, running about the house attempting to create enough agitation to disrupt the impasse of air. I was alone and becoming increasingly anxious with thoughts of such an inauspicious death. I ran out the front door, thinking I might make it to a neighbor's house, when the blockage cleared. I dropped to a sitting position on the steps, still vibrating with fear, which gradually shifted to gratitude for a single breath. The sacred ordinary flowed back and forth with each inhalation and exhalation. I wondered what it would take to sustain gratitude for a single breath.

Another example occurred several years ago, when I found myself receiving a gentle and profound call to the sacred ordinary. My wife and I were snuggled into the comfort and warmth of our Tempur-Pedic bed, each absorbed by the literature of his or her choice. Suddenly, I felt Connie's hand on my shoulder, which I interpreted as a simple gesture of affection. I smiled in recognition of her offering, while remaining focused on the page in front of me.

"Take me with you," she said softly.

"Honey, I'm not going anywhere," I responded, excessively literalizing her ordinary remark and continuing to read.

"I want to go with you," she petitioned again. This time my confusion pulled me away from my book in her direction.

"Connie, what's wrong?" I asked, noticing her tears.

"I want you to take me with you," she replied, getting my attention on a deeper level.

"Tell me where it is you want to go with me," I encouraged, increasingly understanding she was referring to somewhere other than a trip in the neighborhood.

"I want to go to where your vision is calling you," she explained, her words gently gripping my heart as my arms reached out to hold her as they had never held a woman before.

Connie's ordinary words, "Take me with you," were blanketed with the sacred. Her plea sacrificed all pretense, willing to honor my vision and courageously join me. She was also willing to take on the spiritual task of walking close to me while vigilantly remaining loyal to her own vision.

Sacrificing

An old meaning of the word *sacred* is "to sacrifice." When we make the ordinary sacred, something needs to be sacrificed. In Connie's case, she sacrificed a level of pretense that would have rendered her an exaggerated sense of autonomy, suggesting a satisfactory self-reliance. Or she could have witnessed my vision as nothing different from something to be encountered while watching her favorite program on television.

We often need to sacrifice a pompous posturing when the ordinary is deemed a waste of our time and energy. As mentioned earlier, seekers can be easily seduced by the ideal and its promise of something more glamorous. There also may be a more insidious seduction needing our attention. By pursuing what is deemed exemplary and special, we may be invested in our pursuit, suggesting we are also special. Surely, from this seduction, we are not enough of a poet to call forth the riches of the ordinary. Becoming enough of a poet will likely call for a devotion to simplicity.

Simplicity

Simplicity can easily elude the best efforts of the seeker. Hence, what is being quested may be nearby and missed. An old meaning of the word *simplicity* is "singleness of nature." In other words, some one object or thought gets our attention and we allow it to remain there. We are of a single nature when we are focused. We pause, allowing this one focus to impact us. Simplicity does not imply simplemindedness. We may become focused upon some complex consideration by maintaining a singleness of nature and not allowing ourselves to be distracted.

Eliminating distraction in any given moment allows us to live with focus and simplicity. We can take on the task of living with less distraction by bringing more mindfulness to our propensity to be distracted. Some of the following questions can support such mindfulness:

- When am I most easily distracted?
- Do I need the support of firmer boundaries in order to help me remain focused and less distracted?
- Do my distractions help me to avoid feeling some particular emotion?
- Do I get the feeling I'm going to miss something if I resist the distraction?
- Do I feel more productive when I allow myself to be distracted?

When our singleness of focus is accompanied by gratitude or devotion, we engender a spirit of grace. We have elegantly moved into place, the place we belong. No longer laboring to be somewhere else, we are, in a real way, at home.

Our imagination can point us in new directions toward unexplored territory. We can employ the motif of Hermes, the Greek messenger, to help us gain an increased comfort with movement and exploration. In a number of ways, we can follow Hermes home.

A Blessing for Imagination

Imagination is a sacred opening, naturally suited to seekers. It is an open door welcoming passage out and away from a mediocrity wedded to convention. The door flies open, allowing in a breeze awakening us, now an inner voice audible, once deafened by the clamor of an eagerness to fit in.

Imagination is driven by a ruthlessness, fighting for what lies within, giving rise to new eyes and new ears. This tension hungers for new vision. It is your birthplace, the place where you are invited to create yourself again and again. The fullness of the imaginal opening is asking for new and stronger ways of loving. Old ways of carrying heart fall into hands either excessively open to harsh winds or closefisted, leaving the heart with a murmured beat. There is a heart's knowing one that can imagine into a strength of tenderness, a softness of will, and a knowing of when to open and when to close.

Imagination lives by a curiosity animated with an eagerness to know and accompanied by a fullness of care. Only then do seeking and imagining become intimate. In such depth of connection we can welcome our confusion, no longer bowing shamefully as carriers of unknowing.

Imagination is welcomed by wonder. We become more familiar with the seduction of certainty. We can finally feel the distortion and cramping of our assuredness. Repetition begins to lose its pleasantness, replaced by an affection for the limitless.

Imagination is blessed by novelty and creativity. The novel invites us to allow for surprise as it would fall upon a child's eyes—resting upon a matured innocence we call gratitude and awe. The creative moment is ushered in by a pause, allowing our suffering, our longing, and our fears to inseminate our experience. We consummate our relationship to the seen and unseen worlds again and again in a love story meant to live in destiny.

Imagination leans into the sacred ordinary, comfortable in a faith that the face of the ordinary will be revealed with a new and alluring countenance. When simplicity is devotionally carried, imagination comes to know a grace we call home.

5

Following Hermes Home

It is in his [Hermes's] nature not to belong to any locality and not to possess any permanent abode; always he is on the road between here and yonder.

—Walter F. Otto

AS SEEKERS, WE NEED AN image that can support the energy of sustained movement and some deeper understanding of belonging. The image of Hermes may be that image. Hermes is often depicted adorning his traveler's cap, prepared to hit the road. The challenge is to shed some light on home as something other than a permanent abode, and the place of non-permanence in our pursuit of belonging.

These topics are the focus of this chapter, along with how Hermes facilitates our movement as seekers. When we find ourselves being coddled by lethargy and the mundane, we might be duly disturbed by Hermes. The energy of Hermes provides a restlessness and an agitation that can bring curiosity and wonder back into our lives. Animated by these forces, we can realign ourselves with our destiny as seekers.

The Starting Place

Home is where we start from.
                                        —T.S. Eliot

What does it mean to say home is where we start from? We can understand a place we start from as the place where movement begins. If home is where we start from, is the seeker being asked constantly to leave home?

In an earlier chapter, we cited two old meanings of the word *home*, one being "where we choose to linger." Lingering is not a permanent act. It was suggested that we linger because a soul feeding occurs at the place where we remain for a while. The feeding may happen because there's beauty to witness, there's intimacy and relatedness to experience, or simply because we're touched and moved at this place of lingering.

A key here will be not to excessively literalize the image of a place. It may be a physical location; however, seekers are internal pilgrims. Hence, these places of lingering may include beliefs, values, dreams, visions, longings, and deep emotions.

The gift of Hermes's energy may be that lingering and restlessness can easily accompany one another. Lingering suggests a Hermetic attachment to non-permanence, accompanied by restlessness. Lingering is also about pausing and allowing for incubation. It is a time to "take in" on a deeper level. Without taking in a new belief or image, any restlessness becomes a bit suspect. Movement begins to feel somewhat chaotic and aimless, rather than a genuine seeking to add more depth to what is presently being considered.

How do we know when incubation has actually birthed something that is familiar and personal? The second old definition of the word *home*, "familiar and personal," may be a valuable indicator. How can we tell when some way of thinking or some behavior we identify as important to us is familiar and personal? That knowledge comes from a feeling of loss that lets us know we have an intimate relationship with what we believe or value. Similar to being distanced from a friend or lover whom we yearn to connect with, we feel the loss when our lives are not reflecting our deep beliefs. Feeling lost is also an indication we have likely stepped away from what gives our lives value and meaning. We know then that there is something deeply personal we either have wandered away from or are preparing to receive.

Witnessing what touches and moves us suggests that what we see lives in us in a familiar and personal way. Recently, while facilitating work I identify as Dramatic Ritual or Psychodrama, I felt touched and moved as one man in our group courageously encountered a demon from the past.

"I want to do a piece of work," said George, who was rehabbing from a recent knee replacement.

"OK, where do you want this work to focus?" I asked.

"Well, one day while I was in rehab, I awoke in my darkened room and felt myself back in my bedroom as a kid when my father had just finished beating me," George recounted, his eyes wide with a locked vigilance, prompted by an anticipation of an incoming assault.

George went on to explain the terror he had experienced lying in the dark of his bedroom, frightened to cry, as that would typically bring on more brutality. The same terror had revisited him during his rehab stay some fifty years later.

"Well, what would you like to see happen if you step into this work now?" I asked.

"I guess I'm locked into doing something at this point," suggested George.

"Locked in? Oh no, you can stop now after having shared with us the story of what resurfaced for you while in rehab," I added, aware of how trapped he had felt in childhood.

"You mean I have choices right now? I can simply step away from doing something next?" George asked, in disbelief.

"Yes, that's exactly what I mean. There's nothing in this moment you have to do," I explained, noticing that I had no attachment to George doing the work in some particular way.

"Wow! That feels really different. I think I would like to step in and see what I can do with the abused child that lives in me," George said, his facial muscles softening.

"What would you like to see happen in this work?" I asked.

"I want to see if I can create some kind of relationship with that abused kid."

George asked a man in the room to play the role of his inner abused child. The man stood some six feet in front of him. George displayed as much unease as he did gratitude for the appearance of this deeply wounded part of himself.

"George, this is the part of you who lived in terror, could not find his voice, and felt deeply alone," I suggested.

"Yes, no one helped him—not a relative, teacher, policeman, or clergy. He was completely alone!"

"What do you want to say to this child?" I asked.

"Are you willing to trust me?"

"Fuck, no!" came back the exuberant response from the man playing his abused child.

"I want to protect you," George offered, with an endearing tone.

"I never felt very protected," responded the child surrogate.

I intervened, "Well, it seems to me that George has been doing pretty well at taking care of you over these past fifty years. I mean, you're here, looking relatively healthy and comfortable."

Both George and the child surrogate agreed that George had done his best to create safety for this abused kid, who trusted almost no one. I could feel some psychic opening happening between the two.

"I'll continue doing my best to protect you, and if what I'm doing doesn't work for you, let me know and I'll change it. Right now, I would just like to hold you," George offered, which seemed to create a thread of rapport in their relationship.

The child surrogate was willing, and George proceeded to gently hold his abused-child-self with a palpable feeling of care and protection. For a moment there was a quieting of the vibration of George's severe vigilance, as we all witnessed fifty years of an internal fracture. A few stones were being removed from the wall George had built, separating him from the most vulnerable part of himself. We watched as the man who had been a traumatized child dared to allow a man's arms to hold him, trusting for the first time that these arms might not bruise, thrash, and batter.

I sat there touched and moved, witnessing some measure of inner reconciliation that lives at the heart of all healing. I was in the presence of what is deeply familiar and personal, constituting home, or my starting point. One way movement could begin would be to live close to the question, what is this inner reconciliation asking for? Of course, as the person offering a container for the healing, it serves me to ask, what is asking for reconciliation within me?

Movement as Home

It is extremely seductive to attribute permanence to home and to our experience of belonging. Authentic feelings of belonging feel so good, comforting, and reassuring that we do not want them to end. We want where we belong to continue forever. We can certainly linger in such places, allowing our souls a deep feeding, making our experience familiar and personal. However, if where we linger is the place we start from, then we will need the energy of Hermes to understand how our beginning to move can also be familiar and personal. It is crucial for the seeker to come to know movement as deeply personal.

Master of Movement

We do not customarily think of a beginner as a master. Yet no one is more familiar or has a more personal relationship with movement than the novice or beginner. We can get some insight regarding movement that is familiar and personal from the following quote by the Austrian poet Rainer Maria Rilke: "If the angel deigns to come, it will be because you have convinced her, not by tears but by your humble resolve to be always beginning: to be a beginner."

Old meanings of the word *resolve* include "to loosen or undo," and "firmness of purpose." In order to allow ourselves to move into more feeling and more curiosity and wonder, as well as toward taking some risks, we will likely need to loosen some way we've grown accustomed to protecting our hearts and minds. We can see Hermetic movement in the act of loosening.

Three common forms of heart-and-mind protection include: emotional distancing, adapting, and dominating. *Emotional distancing* takes place when we do not disclose how we feel or what we want. We *adapt* by ignoring what we feel and want, taking our lead from the expectations of others. We *dominate* by attempting to influence and recruit others to take on our expectations and beliefs, ignoring their own. There's nothing strange about being able to distance, adapt, and step in and take over. The three strategies constrict movement when they are employed in the extreme. When amped up, they do not allow for the exchange of vision, warmth, and sweetness.

George was willing to undo the distance he had created with the battered part of himself and accept being a beginner at the task of creating rapport with the most fragile piece of his soul. We all could feel the firmness of purpose he displayed in regard to healing a painful past. He possessed the resolve to remain a beginner.

Rilke tells us that the resolve to be a beginner must be humble. We can think of humility as the gracious acceptance of limits. "To be always a beginner" suggests a willingness to remain in relationship with unlimited possibilities. It is this humility to remain a beginner that makes beginning familiar and personal, reflecting a compassionate relationship with our limits.

Hermes points us toward beginning as home. He calls to us for an ego deflation, reminding ourselves we are pursuers of truth, not owners of truth. It is said about Hermes that he has no attachment to falsity or truth. His message is simply his experience, denoting no obsession with drawing conclusions. He remains in pursuit.

It is a humble resolve that blesses seeking as home, displaying a firmness of purpose with no ultimate destination. The gift the seeker receives is remaining on the journey, and to be such is to stay in a personal relationship with the immensity of what is. There may be no greater spiritual task than to remain devoted to a personal relationship with the infinite. It is to shift from the regality of an ego obsessed with knowing to the simplicity of curiosity and wonder characteristic of a beginner. Embracing being a novice calls for a humble resolve to deconstruct an attachment to heroism.

Deconstructing Heroism

In his book *Death of a Hero, Birth of the Soul*, John Robinson refers to the losses we endure when getting attached to being heroic: "What is missing in the original wonder of life, the natural self he once knew long ago, the wounds he buried along the way, and the gifts he is here to realize? He is missing his soul."

Heroism does not allow for the decampment and journeying of Hermes. As Robinson points out, we are taken hostage by the fugitive conspiracy of a denied wound. Heroes become rigidly fixated in a self-righteous set of beliefs, no longer able to wonder and celebrate all that life offers them. The hero occupies a position of protesting non-permanence, therefore protesting change as the essential feature of life. The heroic is not focused on making peace with life but rather conquering it. Such posturing is a setup for unnecessary failure and great disillusionment.

It may be helpful to outline some of the forfeitures that act as impediments to Hermetic movement:

- *Denial of limits* lends itself to getting caught in a web of perfectionism, guaranteeing unnecessary failures and obstructing movement resulting from focusing on what is actually in our control.

- *Attachment to being impressive* gives a good deal of power to the audience, who may or may not respond favorably to our performances. Striving to impress leaves the hero externally referenced, drifting away from the inner core from where personal guidance emanates. The loss of such direction impedes clear and focused action. The hero becomes dependent on external approval, struggling to move toward some valued undertaking while being distracted by "who's noticing."

- *Adversarial relationship with humanity* prevents heroes from accepting the ordinary sacredness of their uniqueness as they strive to be special. This striving inhibits movement toward deeper truths and expressions of compassion. Rejecting their own humanity typically leaves them severely critical of the humanity of others.

- *Denial of non-permanence* happens as an attachment to being heroic pulls us away from our limits into some quixotic vision of "forevering." Such a future orientation replaces living in the moment, where we can actually take on the responsibility of moving into deeper levels of character development.

- *Being condemned to being alone* happens as the hero becomes obsessed with demonstrating a variety of alleged competencies. Vision of the gifts, accomplishments, and needs of others becomes distorted by the heroic mission of conquering and indulging in the illusion of mastering life. Emotional isolation prevails, except during the right times to attempt to rescue and save someone. The ability to move into deeper levels of connection with folks is stalled out.

- *Being doomed to victimization* occurs as the hero steps into situations driven by lofty aspirations but stripped of any likelihood of success. Over time the hero's coping mechanisms grow thin, leaving him unable to creatively carry defeat. The natural result is a propensity to define himself as a victim of people, places, and things. Movement into reliable expressions of personal empowerment is forestalled by blame and claims of a victim's helplessness.

A Cornucopia of Movement

If seekers can loosen their attachment to being heroic, then they can remain focused upon what is in their control rather than attempting to leap tall buildings in a single bound. Once ready to release the impossible, the seeker can more freely move. Hermes, often depicted with winged sandals, offers the seeker the most helpful of biddings: "Be ready to move."

Constant movement is what life and the seeker have in common. The non-permanence of life means life is constantly moving and changing. The seeker is forever stepping onto uncharted territory. Hence, the seeker may find home as a place to linger, feeling gratitude for such a discovery. However, home for the seeker is also making movement personal.

Movement is made personal by claiming it, feeling the importance of it. It is a knowing that our lives are strongly calling for such movement. When movement is deeply personal, it doesn't feel chosen. Rather, we experience a call that cannot be ignored. My friend John recently recounted such a personal movement.

"You know I started up that new project at the church I told you about," John told me.

"Yes, you seemed excited and ready to take it on," I responded.

"Well, I was very excited. I knew several thousand men who would likely want to get involved. I contacted them, and only one man stepped forward to join me—which initially broke my heart," he said, his sadness palpable.

"That had to be challenging for you, since you have been connected with a lot of those guys for a number of years."

"It was very challenging, and after carrying a broken heart for a while, I noticed that the incident had hurt my pride—hurt my pride a lot. So I decided to move closer to finding out how much pride governs my life. I know it is absolutely necessary for me to get clearer about this pride thing," John said with conviction.

"How's your exploration with pride going?" I asked.

"I like it. The other day a man was asking about a particular choice I had made with the project. I noticed that at times my response was clear and soft. Suddenly, a certain intensity came into my voice, suggesting that I felt the need to demonstrate that my choice was legitimate. There was the voice of pride! I was glad to see it. I just know that this move to bring pride into the light will be a great service to my life."

John was teaching me about the deeply personal nature of movement. His heart was strongly involved in the pursuit of his pride. And there was no fanfare. He shared his commitment with his spouse and me. There was an intimacy about his story, an openness to the teachers who would support his quest. We both knew that opportunities to explore his relationship with pride would abound.

Movement from the Unconscious to Consciousness

It may be helpful to cite some of the movements into which Hermes can escort the seeker. As a messenger, Hermes delights in bringing news from one world to another. He's a networker, and one of his delights is bringing information from the unconscious world to consciousness. Hermes has the competency to make this kind of delivery. However, being skilled is not the big deal. We access the gifts of Hermes when we delight in bringing the images and meanings of one world to another. Hermetic delight must lie at the heart of all seekers.

Two Hermetic pathways from the unconscious to consciousness are dreams and projections. *Dreams* can be thought of as the subterranean poetry of the psyche. We can commit to tracking our dreams, writing them down, talking about them, and exploring their images. We can begin by asking, What image in the dream seems to demand my attention? What feelings are aroused by this image? What does the image remind me of?

It can be quite informative to describe an image as concretely and as literally as you can. A simple example would be a dream I had about my bicycle being stolen. I started by asking, what is a bicycle? I responded by saying that it was something you sat on that moved you. You use it to propel yourself forward in a self-empowering way, and you utilize your own body to make it happen. I then worked with the image, wondering if the Hermetic message might be that somewhere in my life, I was allowing my self-empowerment to be stolen. Or perhaps there was some place where I was being excessively dependent.

The second form of delivery is *projections*, which are stories we assign to the subterranean land of the psyche, the unconscious. These narratives are alive and well yet forgotten in the realm of the unconscious. We forget these stories because allegedly they are about some aspect of ourselves we deem unlovable. Examples of what might be called negative themes banished and forgotten include arrogance, insensitivity, self-centeredness, cruelty, ruthlessness, jealousy, and remorselessness.

Sometimes, the themes are more positive; however, if we decide they make some significant people in our lives uncomfortable, potentially jeopardizing their acceptance, these aspects of ourselves may get relegated to the underworld. Examples of these banished positive traits might include intelligence, beauty, cleverness, imagination, intuition, and creativity.

These unconscious stories, positive and negative, take on a life of their own in the unconscious. That is, if we refuse to claim them, our egos will project them onto others. We might not only decide that someone is arrogant but also find ourselves overly focusing on that person's alleged arrogance. We can open to a delivery from Hermes by asking the following questions: Have I projected a story of arrogance onto this particular person? How challenging is it to acknowledge that this story is actually about me? What will it take to reclaim this story as being about me? Can I accept that with self-compassion, so that pulling back the projection will actually serve me?

Seekers benefit greatly from the Hermetic movement from the unconscious to consciousness by remaining self-examining. It is self-examination that allows seekers to genuinely identify what is calling them and what is needed to support the pilgrimage.

Movement from Heart to Brain and Back Again

> One ought to hold on to one's heart; for if one lets it go,
> one soon loses control of the head too.
> —Friedrich Nietzsche

In another of my titles, I included a photograph of the heart of a twenty-four-day-old fetus creating brain cells. We apparently begin this journey with such a heart, seeking attachment, closeness, acceptance, and love. Most of us have some experience with warmth, tenderness, and deep emotional comfort. What a great place to linger and call home! Yet strong heart sentiment tends to become an insulator, closing out that which might disturb the tranquility of heartfelt nesting.

Strong sentiment needs the mind's curiosity and wonder in order to support seeking. Jack Kornfield describes it this way:

> The unawakened mind tends to make war against the way things are. To follow a path with heart, we must understand the whole process of making war within ourselves and without, how it begins and how it ends. War's roots are in ignorance. Without understanding we can easily become frightened by life's fleeting changes, the inevitable losses, disappointments, the insecurity of our aging and death. Misunderstanding leads us to fight against life, running from pain or grasping at security and pleasures that by their nature can never be satisfying.

Kornfield suggests that a mind at war has not likely listened to its own frightened and insecure heart. Hermes can guide our minds back into a mind-heart conversation. Is the belief I hold driven by some fear or insecurity? What do I fear? What is this fear asking for? Is my fear asking me to act in a way that is incongruent with my values? What do I need to do in order to feel my fear and feel safe doing so? What does accessing viable support for feeling insecure look like in this situation?

Movement from heart to mind and back again allows for peace to come to two wars: the heart's war on what could be and the mind's war on what is.

Movement from the Rational to the Transrational

It is in keeping with the spirit of Hermes not to get too abstract about abstract concepts like "rational" and "transrational." What typically is needed to identify a belief as rational? The most popular way we determine a belief to be *rational* depends upon collecting data through observation. This is called inductive reasoning, which happens when we experience some event happening over and over again and then draw a particular conclusion about the future occurrence of that event. An example would be to observe the sun rising in southeastern Connecticut by 7:00 a.m. throughout the year and then predicting the sun will rise tomorrow by 7:00 a.m. in southeastern Connecticut. This kind of rational thought deals with probability—that is, what is likely to occur based upon past observation.

What information we deem rational or reasonable often reflects a yearning, and sometimes we desperately want to be in possession of the truth to be right. Without Hermes's guidance supporting new explorations and imagining, we can easily fall prey to believing that our beliefs can be stripped of ambiguity. It serves us well to remember that the rational cannot take us all the way home to absolute truth. Our humanity is destined to embrace a kinship with an approximation of the truth.

Our reasoning can be easily comforted when it is supported by consensus. However, having the gang on our side can be encouraging and, at times, very limiting. For example, it does seem to behoove us to pay attention when over ten thousand scientists claim that humans are contributing to climate change through carbon emissions. However, it was the consensus in the fourteenth century that the sun revolved around the earth. Science got a boost when Galileo stepped out of the box and contended that the Earth revolved around the sun. Part of Galileo's hypothesis was based on observation, likely accompanied by intuition and imagination. The transrational is typically not supported by consensus. To hold a transrational view may therefore call for more courage than brilliance.

The *transrational* is expressed in poetry, music, art, drama, dreams, ritual, imagination, and intuition. A transrational belief does not rely upon a collection of data and evidence. Hence, the transrational becomes very important when exploring those aspects of the human condition not easily supported by observation. Our vision of justice, freedom, love, God, beauty, courage, devotion, compassion, and creativity are amongst those human endeavors deeply in need of the transrational.

Recently, I told my friend Tim that the way he had accompanied his father's dying had made a significant contribution toward bringing a measure of peace to the planet. As you'll see in his story, the amount of heart he was able to bring to the process was a clear example of the transrational.

Tim's father had terrorized his wife and four children with an unrestrained reign of harshness and brutality. He routinely bullied, intimidated, and beat his family. Yet Tim showed up at his father's bedside during hospice care with a devotion to maintain a caring vigil during his father's last days. He spoke to his father about the few sweet times the family had known. He caressed his head and regularly bathed him. Tim was neither in denial of this man's ruthlessness, nor was he stuck somewhere in childhood desperately attempting to secure some last-minute paternal approval. Instead, Tim was choosing to participate in his father's dying with an offering of nurturing hands, hands possessing the power to transform the force of a dying man's fists. The brute of a man Tim called Father could no longer rage against a tender moment. It was time for Tim to exercise his will, bringing compassion and sweetness to a rapport both were starving for.

Tim gently placed a warm cloth on his father's eyes, washing away a crust of sleep, a crust of life that had hardened for a long time. Tim's eyes welcomed his father's gaze into a soft light, allowing the old man to see a son walking with him into his last days. Tim rinsed the cloth again, tenderly wiping the drool from his father's chin, where once spittle had frothed over from a boiling ferocity.

Tim placed moisturizing lotion in his hands and gently messaged each of his father's fingers in a ritual-like motion. Each stroke appeared to possess the power to release his father's hands of a tension that had lost its usefulness long ago. Tim seemed to know that each caress welcomed his father to rest in the comfort of the late winter of his life. The old man had returned to the need, the dependency, and the vulnerability of infancy—all of which he had raged war against his entire life. Tim was glad to escort his father back to himself.

One of the distinctions between the rational and the transrational is that while the former is typically ego driven—"I'm exploring," "I'm deciding," "I'm searching," and "I'm believing"—the transrational tends to place us more into the position of being told, being informed, and being instructed. So it was for me to be in the presence of Tim's story.   Every detail and pause in Tim's narrative told me I was hearing a story for the first time. Not just Tim's story—this was a story about fathering, cruelty, kindness, courage, and redemption that lacked any hidden psychological agenda. As I sat listening to Tim's account of those last days with his father, I had the increased sensibility that I was not simply listening. Rather, I was being informed.

When I finally was able to name the instruction, I said, "What you gave your father was an immense offering of peace, not only to him but to the entire planet." Of course, there was no way to prove or demonstrate the truth of my utterance, but it resonated throughout my entire being. To this day, I believe Tim continues to attempt to make sense of my comment, as do I.

Another more personal example of the transrational happened to me in 1999. My wife Connie was a fervent believer in astrology, while I maintained a level of skepticism. She asked if I would be willing to have her lifelong friend do my astrological chart. I agreed and was willing to learn more about this ancient art form to which my spouse had been a devotee.

As we traveled to a suburb of Boston in order to receive my reading, Connie pointed out that Rania was not only an accomplished astrologer but that she also possessed some psychic ability. The characterization of her friend intrigued me.

Some ninety minutes later, we parked in front of a large brown-and-green Victorian home. We ascended the stairs of a wide wraparound porch and rang the doorbell. Rania—dressed casually with a white blouse with turned-up collar and green cotton slacks—quickly opened the door, standing somewhat stoically, with no verbal welcome. Her eyes remained as large as the gems strung along a necklace that demanded attention. Her body, positioned in the doorway, resembled that of a bouncer at a nightclub. Her gaze remained distant, revealing a striking incongruence with what it might mean to greet an old friend.

Finally, Connie broke the silence and asked if we could come in. Rania slowly backed away and led us through glass doors opening to a parlor with bay windows, two matching gray easy chairs, and a brown sofa. The awkwardness of the initial greeting continued to hang in the room. I comforted myself by scanning the surroundings, noticing a large mirror above the fireplace, a painting of an old barn on a snowy winter day on my right, and a blue-and-gold Persian rug under my feet.

Rania looked toward me and interrupted the silence by asking "Do you have any significant resistance to experiencing this reading?"

"When I drive ninety minutes and am willing to miss a Patriots' game, I likely don't have heavy resistance to whatever I'm attending," I explained confidently.

"Well, I put your numbers together, and over and over again I could not access any real meaning. I just kept visioning an iron door," Rania declared, with a note of frustration.

"I'm afraid I can't explain your experience," I added.

"What do you know about Mystery schools?" asked Rania, inquiring about something I had never heard about.

"You shouldn't be talking this way!" I blurted out, having no idea why I said what I had just said.

"I figured. He continues to carry the many vows he took while participating in various Mystery schools," Rania commented, directing her remarks to Connie.

"I told you that you should not be talking like this," I yelled aggressively, completely bewildered about the source of my words.

I then began to sob uncontrollably, while Rania explained that a reading could not take place on this day. Connie drove us home as I continued to experience what appeared to be deep grief, with no understanding about the nature of these strong emotions.

For a number of years I carried a mild curiosity about Mystery schools, but the incident at Rania's prevented any serious investigation. Thirteen years later I became interested in the life of the sixth-century BCE philosopher Pythagoras. Although I had studied Western philosophy for many years, I had no understanding of this seminal figure, other than his contributions to the field of geometry. I learned that he had spent twenty-two years studying in the Mystery schools of Alexandria and that following his study with the Magi of Persia, he began identifying himself as a "lover of Sophia."

The first time I saw the words "lover of Sophia," my entire body vibrated and I wanted to yell, "Me too! I am a lover of Sophia!" I had no idea what it meant to be a lover of Sophia, yet I could not escape the grip of knowing that those words constituted the strongest way of describing myself. I knew who I was in a strange and unexplainable way.

I continue to wonder about myself as a lover of Sophia, and if Hermes permits, I will add to my initial interpretations, which include these: lover of wisdom, lover of seeking, lover of heart knowing, and lover of wonder. But most of all, a lover of Sophia is willing to live the questions pertaining to the nature of love and the nature of wisdom.

I learned that Pythagoras went to Southern Italy and created a Mystery school at the town of Croton. In 2013 I created the Croton Mystery School, resulting from the strange musings that had occurred fourteen years earlier in Rania's parlor, where I was deeply touched by the transrational.

Movement between Worlds

Hermes is often depicted wearing winged sandals, facilitating his movement from one world to another. We can think of four different worlds corresponding to the four elements: air, water, earth, and fire. Seekers are in need of Hermes's versatility. Seekers can ask these questions: Which world offers me the greatest comfort? Which world do I typically criticize, possibly denoting my resistance to visit that world? Which world do I fear? What world is asking for my curiosity and exploration? What happens to my capacity to seek when I get enamored with one world?

Let's look at each world through the lens of that world's contribution to seeking, the potential seduction of getting stuck in that world, and how Hermes assists movement.

The World of Air

The world of air literally provides us with breath and is invisible. We live in this invisible exchange, with trees sending us oxygen as we send back the carbon dioxide they need. To breathe is to inspire. The metaphor of air can inspire through new ideas, intuition, and vision. The activity of minds is the clearest metaphor for the world of air, occupied by reflection, beliefs, and opinions. The world of air provides us with the opportunity to create our own ideas, to give serious consideration to the thinking presented to us by former thinkers, the media, friends, and colleagues. Wind literally provides us with power as it moves windmills, and so it is with new and evocative ideas that can empower revolutionary change. The essential gift of the world of air may be its dedication to lessening ignorance.

> Now whether it be
> Bestial oblivion, or some craven scruple

Of thinking too precisely on th'event—
A thought which, quarter'd, hath but one part wisdom
And ever three parts coward—I do not know
Why yet I live to say this thing's to do,
Sith I have cause, and will, and strength, and means
To do't.
(Shakespeare, *Hamlet*)

The essential seduction of this world is to become anesthetized by air. We can see in the above quote from *Hamlet* the inherent challenge to move from air to embodied action. It will be helpful to explore how the delirium of air takes place with a strong alluring.

When we take up residency in this world, we think, think, and think. One idea produces another, and like a hot-air balloon, we begin to lift off the ground, distancing ourselves from the flow of waters and blazing fires. Similar to actual air, we become invisible, hidden amongst the clouds of cerebral enchantment. Distant from the ground, our sense of presence loses its rhythm, tonality, and timbre. We become like a breeze, experienced with no location, origin, or destination.

If we can bring some ground to air, then we can cool the air through condensation. Condensation happens as we bring more ground to our experience. This can happen by more attention to deep breathing, focusing on our feet connected to the earth, and tracking both internal and external sensations. As condensation occurs, vapor, or excessive thinking, turns into water. We can return to the flow of our emotional lives.

Hermes, traveling between worlds, can inform us regarding our losses when stuck in one world. Hermes's message might include what it means to be removed from water. We run the risk of our felt experience drying up; grief is desiccated, with sorrow, sadness, and pain becoming arid. We lose the capacity to have our waters erode blockage and clean, fill, and clear what weighs heavy upon our hearts. Air lovers take on an alleged immunity from a broken heart.

The air dweller can easily disconnect from fire, losing a capacity for warmth and passion. Being anesthetized by air numbs our longing and our loving as we strive to be impervious to rejection and hurt.

The seeker suffers several significant losses when drugged by air. When the seeker is seduced by air, movement is sacrificed. She is an injured pilgrim, severely hampering a quest for the sacred. She can no longer be guided by the energies of the other three worlds. She cannot benefit from questions like these: What felt experience would enhance my idea? What risks are my beliefs requesting? What passion calls me to some lived experience where my soul would be fed? What information does my heart have for my mind?

Falling prey to the seduction of air is popular. Air residents are often admired for their intellectual prowess and can easily become dependent upon a world enamored of their intellectual musing. There is also something deeply comforting and potentially destructive about deciding "I don't have to live life, I can think about it."

The World of Water

The contribution of the world of water is largely the capacity to live with heart. Water allows us seekers to grieve our losses, enabling us to let go and move on. Deep feeling makes significant contributions to what gives our lives meaning, what's worth living and dying for. Water is the sustenance of a thriving heart. Seekers gain great benefit from knowing what they love and doing what they can do to live their love. Heart waters tell us how love lives in us, how we need it to come from us and to us. These waters can bring compassion to what we believe, expanding our vision and affording us the chance to live in larger stories. When these waters are aerated, these stories may be less constricted by revenge, pride, and a need to be right.

In C.S. Lewis's classic Christian satire *The Screwtape Letters*, an elder demon writes to a young demon about how to lead a particular man astray so that the man will eventually lose his soul. In one letter, Screwtape writes of this man, "The more often he feels without acting, the less he will be able ever to act, and in the long run, the less he will be able to feel." Lewis reminds us here of the connection between water and earth, with our feelings yielding more action and our action stimulating a richer emotional life. However, when the seduction of water remains, life can be deeply felt but not lived. Drowned in sentiment, we are convinced that feeling accepted, understood, and loved is what really matters. But Hermes, the traveler between worlds, can inform us that when floodwaters rise in the world of water, the ground under our feet erodes, fires of ambition are doused, and the winds of inspiration and change go ignored.

Hermes can bring a souvenir of fire in the form of a care package to the world of water. Gifts would include desire, longing, passion, ambition, and anger. Under the influence of this heat, water begins to evaporate into vapor or air. The torrent of emotional outpouring can then subside, replaced by clearer thinking and greater vision.

The World of Earth

> *It turns out that people who are grounded and secure don't change much under stress. That's what being grounded means.*
>
> —Michael Gruber, *The Good Son*

The world of earth gives us ground, allowing us to be fully present in one place. Having firm ground under our feet opens us to being enlivened by our senses. When we are grounded, we are ready to receive information about the world around us. Grounding also helps us to be receptive to internal sensations, making us aware of what is occurring inside us—tightening in different bodily locations, as well as temperature changes. The gift of ground contributes to our being more visible and accessible to others. Building solid rapport with others calls for being solidly grounded, which announces our presence and capacity to be engaged.

Ground offers rootedness, making us less vulnerable to external forces such as influence, expectations, and demands. Gruber's quote above points to both the strength and weakness of ground. We are not so easily uprooted; however, too much ground can dam the flow of changing waters, leading to stagnation. The seduction of ground is that the strength of rootedness can suggest we are where we need to be and that there's no need for movement.

Abraham Maslow writes, "You will either step forward into growth, or you will step back into safety." This points out that the grand seduction of ground is accompanied by a grand illusion—that standing still is actually possible! Hence, there is no arrival. We are moving forward with Hermes's guidance or moving back to modes of safety created in childhood. Too much earth, like mountains, can obstruct the flow of air as well as stomp out embers of passion.

The World of Fire

Fire advanced evolution by providing warmth, the ability to cook, and protection from predators. Unlike air, ground, and water, which appear naturally, we learned to create fire, thus giving us a sense of empowerment. Therefore, we took our relationship to fire seriously, learning to create weapons, use gas and oil, and eventually use thermonuclear energy. Our DNA likely carries a memory of the immense contribution fire made to our early empowerment and survival.

On a psychic level, fire offers warmth, passion, and vitality. Air, for example, typically needs fire in order to be truly inspiring. Fire announces our presence and can reveal an intimate kinship with life.

The seduction of fire is the belief that the larger the blaze, the more we are alive. It is so easy to convince ourselves that a large inferno holds so much enthusiasm and animation that it must reflect a large expression of life. However, its excessive intensity moves us away from the nuances of feeling and intuiting. The messages of softer inner voices can go unheard in the face of excess fire. We run the risk of burning our connection to others as we are consumed by our own exuberance, the price being the incineration of empathy.

While I was having coffee with a friend recently, he interrupted some passionate declaration of mine by commenting, "I often find you to be significantly formidable." To him, my articulation of my beliefs carried so much fire that any differing opinion might be torched in the presence of my blaze. My friend made it clear that my intensity made it difficult for him to hear something new from me and then express his own wonderings about it to me. My friend's feedback brought me closer to the importance of grounding my fire, if our conversations were to be co-created. I immediately favored the grounding, since I had not gathered with my friend with the intention of offering a lecture.

When flames are fed, they move up and away from the ground. The intensity of fire removes us from the ground, and that shift obstructs our ability to be present. These flames can singe our threads like connection to the moment.

We all tend to take up residency in the world that most easily accommodates our natural instincts and strengths. The seduction is to attribute powers to that world that are unrealistic. When that happens we are short on growth-producing resources. Ground or earth provides stability, accessibility, and presence. Air offers insight, intuition, and imagination. Water offers the capacity to grieve and experience the softer qualities of sadness, hurt, and vulnerability;

the world of water opens hearts. Fire provides passion, longing, and devotion.

Hermes's Sparking Movement

Hermes travels lightly to each world, bringing messages of each world's potential contribution. Several characteristics of Hermes facilitate the movement necessary to seeking. These aids to action include being undignified, having a propensity to steal, not getting stuck when some event begins, and being a messenger to the realm of the dead—all of which we'll explore here.

Being Undignified

> *We know that Hermes is not a hero; so we have to think of the nymph, because of her close association with him, as having nothing to do with heroism or redemption but as associated with the undignified side of life.*
> —Rafael López-Pedraza, *Hermes and His Children*

The Hermetic characteristic of being undignified is essential to seeking as well as relevant to learning and healing. An attachment to being on an exalted or dignified path easily distracts us from that which we seek. Endless seductions call us to an exalted track. The illusionary escape from our creatureliness is extremely alluring. The ego loves holding the vision of its ability to transcend the human condition, leaving behind all that would diminish some celestial status. A dignified path holds the alleged confirmation of our worthiness. These ego-driven demonstrations may reflect our intellectual plumage or a résumé of sparkling achievements.

There are endless ways calling us to maintain some dignified presentation to the world. It may be that we get caught up in an obsessive need to give to others in the hope that we will be perceived as possessing a dignified and impeccable altruism. Sometimes it results simply from an unwillingness to own darker energies, such as jealously, contempt, and arrogance.

I recently had surgery on my foot, which placed me into an astronaut-like boot and on crutches. As I hobbled down toward the bathroom, I noticed my assistant emerging from the back office. I immediately picked up my pace, hoping to prevent her from noticing my undignified infirmity. *Dignified* denotes distinguished and strong, which my condition disallowed. I still find myself wondering if I can welcome the hurting hobbler. It may be that disability and aging are the great invitations to the undignified core of humanity. Without such invitation, we might remain seduced by something more pretentious and hopefully impressive.

When spiritual leaders, teachers, and healers resist the undignified, they risk obstructing the movement that their purposes call for. When spiritual leaders lean into the exalted, they can easily communicate a holier-than-thou attitude toward those whom they shepherd. Their followers risk getting caught in a web of endless striving toward purification. Teachers who insist upon being dignified send a strong message of being in possession of the truth while their students remain snarled in ignorance.

Healers resisting the undignified can send messages of pathology to their patients, denoting an unfortunate injury. This lofty posturing offers the healer an alleged immunity from human suffering; it prevents the healer from joining the patient in the human experience of a "suffering soul"—the original meaning of the word *pathology*.

In May 2014, Thomas Moore, author of *Care of the Soul*, reminded a group of healers at a colloquium held in Galway, Ireland, of the value of healers' embracing the undignified. Moore pointed out that healers easily slip into a heroic posture when attached to being dignified. Heroism in the therapeutic relationship places emphasis upon the healer being attached to displaying some professional plumage.

Joining clients in the narrative of their wound is thus compromised, with the healer forgetting that all healing comes from within.

Stealing

The myth of Hermes depicts him as stealing his brother's cattle shortly after being born and backing up slowly out of the corral during the theft. We can raise the question of how stealing might facilitate Hermetic movement.

Jill, a fifty-two-year-old nurse with three children, had been focused on her marriage in her work with me. As the narrative of her relationship with her husband unfolded, it became apparent that a significant childhood dynamic was being reproduced in the marriage.

Jill's older brother, Edward, had taken her family of origin hostage. It appeared he was a narcissistic bully who terrorized his two sisters and left his parents baffled as to what to do with him. Her father was highly passive, moving from denial to a quixotic hope that some divine intervention would emancipate the family from the boy's tyranny. Her mother exercised her best efforts to control Edward, which left her feeling more overwhelmed than effective.

Jill was by nature a sensitive and cooperative child. It didn't take much for her to figure out that her gift to her parents would simply be not adding to Edward's unbridled malice. She remained highly adaptive and compliant, setting her up for being the recipient of spousal bullying.

During a session when she was reviewing her childhood, she wanted to bring attention to a specific incident that baffled her.

"I remember being eight years old; my uncle gave me a quarter. I went to the local five-and-dime store and bought a small red ball. What I don't understand is why I went home and hid the ball," she said.

"Did you think that your brother might take it from you? " I asked.

"No, it would not have interested him."

"Maybe you were stealing your desire and wanting the theft to remain a secret," I suggested.

"Why would I need to steal my desire?"

"Well, you were strongly committed to being non-disruptive. It was a significant way for you to love your parents, and your desire would be a potential source of disruption," I pointed out.

"Are you saying that a child's desire is always a potential source of disruption?"

"Absolutely. Nothing holds the power to shake the status quo like desire. It can push against the norms of the group and set up a competing energy with the desires of others," I explained.

"I think I get it. I'm remembering several other times as a young adult when I bought something and hid it, although there were no apparent consequences for revealing my purchases," she recounted, with a fading tone suggesting the weight of her awareness.

"Your commitment to remain non-disruptive demanded that you give your desire away. What you're noticing is that there were times you simply wanted to steal it back."

"Is it possible that my marriage is also asking me to steal my desire and risk being disruptive?" she asked, with a flavor suggesting more knowing than confusion.

I went on to indicate that it is highly likely that each of us has something to steal, something relinquished early on that we need to reclaim. I pointed out that I was not suggesting that we indulge in some cavalier act of thievery but rather steal what we need in order to meet the demands of the journey. It can be some passion, intellectual acuity, talent, or unique personality trait that seems to annoy someone.

Jill began to steal her desire in her marriage by being willing to interrupt her childhood strategy of excessive compliance. She decided she wanted a marriage that accommodated the desire of both her and her spouse, which was a major life decision for her. Her heist began by being willing to authentically say yes and no. She consummated her theft by refusing to be intimidated by her husband's bullying. She was prepared to employ whatever boundary was necessary to adequately protect herself.

Her boundary building called for more thieveries. She needed to steal her self-loyalty. As a child, her loyalty was to the equanimity of the family system. As a woman and a wife, her loyalty would now be a sacred offering she made to herself.

Jill's movement into seeking greater personal empowerment and greater safety, clarifying how she wanted to love and be loved and live more authentically, was facilitated by her willingness to steal her desire. She knew how to regroup when she became distracted. She would create an image of the girl who hid her red ball and would instinctively begin to steal her desire.

If we are to support the necessary movement for seeking, then focusing on what needs to be stolen is critical. Here are some questions meant to assist you in focusing on the object of the heist: What part of myself did I sacrifice for my survival and the alleged greater good of my family? What price have I paid for this sacrifice? How do I concretely steal what I need? What resources will I need in support of this theft? Who are my valued accomplices?

Not Getting Stuck

Shortly after Hermes is born he leaves his mother's cradle and goes to an adjoining mountain where he builds a seven-stringed lyre and begins to sing songs. He then steals Apollo's cattle, kills two cows, and dines. He then returns to his mother's cradle, where he is scolded for his shenanigans. He responds to his mother by saying that if he cannot share in the affluence and honors of the other immortals, then he will choose to become chief of robbers.

We can employ Hermes's postnatal activity as an important metaphor for movement. Rather than letting us get stuck ruminating endlessly upon the birth of a new idea or intention, Hermes guides us into action. We can think of Hermetic guidance as something other than a promotion of imprudence or heedlessly moving forward. Rather, it is simply an intolerance of being stuck. We can also read into his own insistence that he share in the affluence and honors of the other immortals an encouragement to us to steal our own divine spark, thus effecting the reclamation of our souls.

Hermes reminds us of the perils of getting stuck, entangled either in a web of excessive pondering of some possible action or trapped in excessive self-reliance. Typically, it is fear that incarcerates us behind bars of inexhaustible reflection. We fear making a mistake, we fear being wrong, we fear failure, we fear rejection—and most of all, we fear self-admonishment.

Again, we see the benefit of Hermes's attachment to the undignified, which is not a preoccupation with vulgarity. The undignified welcomes the creaturely and non-heroic expressions of the human condition: making mistakes and failing to reflect a willingness to be fully alive. This fullness suggests movement rather than the psychic stagnation hazardous to seeking.

Hermes receives guidance from Mnemosyne (Memory) and divination from three virginal sisters who are depicted as bee-like creatures. Hermes's guidance is not hampered by a compulsive self-reliance, lacking in diverse perspective and encouragement from others. Again, how undignified and non-heroic it is to receive help!

Being a Messenger to the Realm of the Dead

Hermes as messenger to the realm of the dead allows us also to approach depression as a constant level in our

nature. We know the psychic imager[ies] of death and
depression are so akin they often overlap.
  —Rafael López-Pedraza, *Hermes and His Children*

Movement needed by the seeker is impeded when we separate life and death as if they had nothing to do with one another. Hermes's movement from the realm of the living to the realm of the dead and back again reminds us of the inextricable connection between life and death. Let's look at how this messenger to the realm of the dead helps us to be more fully alive.

We can first ask, why travel to the realm of the dead? One response would be to be reminded that non-permanence is the nature of life. It is only too easy to get myopic about our view of *non-permanence*, which simply means we get to die at some point. However, the Hermes message might be larger, suggesting that everything is non-permanent, including this very moment.

This larger consideration of life's non-permanence simply informs us that life is about change and change is about loss. Because we live in a death-denying culture, it is easy to stay deluded about the ubiquitous nature of loss. It's everywhere! As Aeschylus says, "There's nothing certain in a man's life except this: that he must lose it." If we can come out of denial and/or out of protest about life's being so much about loss, we can then move into greater acceptance of life and from that acceptance, live more freely and deeply.

If we choose to access more mileage from the messenger to the realm of the dead, then we can ask questions that help us to be more fully alive, such as, what in my life is asking for a death? Movement is obstructed when we resist or protest some loss, especially those that are out of our control. At sixty-seven, I can move into protesting the loss of youth. My body neither performs nor looks like it did twenty years ago. I wonder if my protest isn't simply my ego crying out, "I'm not helpless over this loss! I won't just allow this aging thing to happen to me! I'll protest it!" Obviously, my protest is an empty and feeble expression of power.

It may be that the greatest challenge in accepting loss is being powerless to stop it. However, if we are willing to deepen our rapport with the messenger to the realm of the dead, we discover he is also the messenger to the realm of the living. Hermes moves freely from one realm to the other. His message from the realm of the living might be to tell us to ask ourselves, what is life asking of me? What risk is appropriate for me to take at this time? What welcome is attempting to make its way into my life? What seeks to be born in my life? Hermes reminds us that *change* is a euphemism for "something dies and something is birthed."

At sixty-seven years old, I find that the death of my youth is asking for my acceptance. The very act of interrupting my protest of the loss of youth means accepting my significant helplessness. I cannot stop this body from aging, and my protest simply places me in an illusion of power. My hope is that an emerging acceptance of my loss might bring me closer to accepting life's impermanence. Could it be that letting go of our protest of loss opens us to life's non-permanence—opening us to more life? Yes—we stop suggesting that life should be something other than what it is. But isn't that exactly what allows us to flourish in any relationship: accepting what is?

Hermes reminds us that depression shares some of death's primary characteristics: vitality, passion, and buoyancy of energy are diminished or lost. Rather than pathologize the loss of these life energies, we can allow the messenger to the realm of the dead to inform us. It is also important to see the realm of the dead expressed in the passivity of depression. We can ask, How might vital psychic energies get depressed, pushed down and away? What is the sleep of depression asking for?

We often experience life as too big to move, with too many expectations to meet, too much defeat, and too much powerlessness. So we collapse, no longer believing we can muster enough energy to meet life's challenges and insecurities. It may be a time to pause and listen to the herald who travels to the realm of the depressed.

The messenger might initially inform you regarding the appropriateness of pausing and depressing your life forces through a series of questions: Have you encountered an expression of life's immensity, compelling you to pause and take inventory? Have you held the idyllic belief that you hold domination and command over life? Are you being asked to clarify what you have and do not have control over? Are you being asked to grieve some loss? Have you accessed supportive resources to help you attend to some task that overwhelms you? Are you being asked to find a new level of courage, needed in order to once again engage life on life's terms?

We have been exploring how this mythic herald, Hermes, can support us to move less encumbered by extraneous distractions. He helps us to define home as a place to linger for renewal, and he teaches us what it means to make movement familiar and personal. Ultimately, it will be our willingness to embrace being a beginner that will allow us to define home as the starting point, again and again.

As we allow ourselves to move with more suppleness, releasing our hold upon rigid ways of creating safety, we can open to the world of enchantment. With Hermetic nimbleness, we can learn to deepen an intimate relationship with life.

A Blessing for Hermes

May the herald of antiquity find his way to your soul.
You will know his presence in a new vision of home.
Home will be the place to linger, feeding your soul.
It will be the starting place for the journey of seeking
to begin.
Home will be an intimacy with movement.

Movement becomes intimate when you embrace the sacredness of being a beginner. Only the beginner has a deep relationship with the immensity of all that is. Adorning Hermes's traveling cap, we delight in stepping into the vastness of the inner and outer worlds.

With Hermes as our muse, we become life's messengers. We are in the service of life, couriers of life's endless images. Now, less preoccupied with drawing conclusions, more eager to bring news of the water of sentiment, the vision of air, the ground of earth, and the passion of fire from one world to another.

Hermes bestows the gift of shedding heroic overtures. No longer tied to valorous endeavors, desire to conquer is replaced by a passion to move—these advances being energized by the sublime gifts of wonder and curiosity.

This courier reminds us of the value of the undignified. We release our attachment to pretense and being impressive. Free now to seek, no longer encumbered by an ego determined to demonstrate its sovereignty. Teaching, healing, and guiding are no longer burdened by lofty testimonials.

This herald would have mind know heart and heart know mind. The poetry of dreams and stories banished to the underworld of the unconscious are welcomed into the light. This messenger binds death with life. His movement is by nature a celebration of the non-permanence of death and the non-permanence of life—we come to know the faces of each.

Oh, mischievous herald! Rascal that you are, delighting in being a sojourner, bringing your experience from here to there. With no excessive attachment to being right, you take in fully one world, bringing your worldliness to another place. Images for arousing curiosity and wonder are your bounty.

6

Seeking Enchantment

The first step in enchantment, then, is to recover a beginner's mind and a child's wonder, to forget some of the things we have learned and to which we are attached.
—Thomas Moore, *The Enchantment of Everyday Life*

THE ENERGY OF LONGING GIVES inspiration to seekers. It is the longing to experience the enchantment of being touched and moved, and the magic of awakening to a new vision. However, we will need to forget or let go of some of the beliefs we have learned in order to live an enchanted life, including the ideas that it is too dangerous to live with an open heart, too dangerous to dream, too dangerous to have our own unique vision, and too dangerous to love deeply. Real or perceived danger has the power to usurp an enchanted life and inhibit the seeker's pilgrimage. We protect ourselves by diminishing access to our hearts, replacing the enchantment of seeking with an attachment to surviving.

As mentioned earlier, the word *wonder* has an old meaning reflecting the word *wonderful*. When we are preoccupied with surviving, life is not experienced as wonderful. There is no enchantment in our lived experience. We are engaged in some measure of struggle in order to provide ourselves with safety. This striving for safety can happen with varying degrees of fighting, fleeing, and freezing. We can say that each of these postures is an attempt to remove our hearts from perceived danger, the dilemma being that the protection they afford easily morphs into disenchantment.

In this chapter, we will initially look at how seekers get stuck in disenchantment, our psyches moving automatically into postures of fighting, fleeing, or freezing. Enchantment depends upon our ability to pause, ground, and calm ourselves. As we are able to feel fear and simultaneously feel safe, we set the stage for enchantment.

Disenchantment

Disenchantment denotes a loss of open-mindedness and heart. We no longer perceive life as wonderful, as a gift deserving of our curiosity, love, and devotion. Life has become something to protect ourselves from. As with any relationship, once we are guarded from life, there is little hope of giving freely or receiving within our relationship to life. When the psyche perceives danger, it exercises a tenacious and relentless defense on behalf of our safety. So often, the defenses employed are more of a hindrance to seekers than is the perceived threat.

There are numerous ways of being traumatized, fostering strong defenses that result in disenchantment. In his seminal work, *In an Unspoken Voice*, Peter Levine explores how a variety of traumas shock and inhibit an open heart and mind. He says, "Other traumas include falls, serious illness, abandonment, receiving shocking or tragic news, witnessing violence, and getting into an auto accident; all can lead to PTSD. These many other fairly common experiences are all potentially traumatizing. . . . Simply, when you perceive threat, your nervous system and body prepare you to kill or to take evasive countermeasures to escape, usually by running away."

Fighting

Fighting is a typical response to feeling threatened. At the extreme, fighting happens violently as an attempt to injure, drive away, or kill a perceived predator. We may also be fighting for something such as social activism or civil rights. When we do not give ourselves the permission to fight, especially where it is appropriate, we run the risk of being traumatized with the aggressive energy being frozen in our nervous system. When that happens, our vital energies become domesticated, losing their wildness. Our passion becomes tamed and we lose the buoyancy needed to support enchantment.

We either avoid the aggressive energy of fighting all together or fight when it is unnecessary. When we do fight, it is typical to assault one another in ways that diminish and alienate, with our relationships losing their enchantment.

Most of us were raised with two culturally condoned ways to fight, especially in reaction to experiencing diverse needs and opinions. The first is the "right-wrong" dynamic, which finds each person armored with reasons demonstrating the correctness of his position while pointing out the lack of credibility in the other's views. The energy exercised in the name of substantiating a particular stance loses the spirit of creativity and exploration characteristic of enchantment. Demonstrating that the views of others are wrong ruptures rapport. A loss of collaboration, play, and co-creation are vivid indicators of disenchantment. The message sent is "I will not honor your position if it is different from mine" or "I will not make intellectual and psychological space for you if we have diverse views."

Another form of fighting is "win-lose." It is similar to the right-wrong method, often with less of the intellectual flair of right-wrong. Loud voices, facial muscles tightening, physical gyrations, and shallow and rapid breath with darting eyes all reflect an intense competitive energy. The intensity is often driven by shame. There is an urgency to defeat an opposing view in order to secure a temporary reprieve from a deep sense of not being enough. Unfortunately, boisterous voices reciting alleged documentation are often perceived as demonstrating confidence rather than revealing a soul riddled with self-loathing.

Recently, a student of mine anxiously approached me regarding a perception she had that was quite incompatible with my own.

"Earlier today, I heard you say our class adjourned early last meeting because of snow," Doris recounted.

"Yes, I remember leaving two hours early because of the snow," I responded.

"Well, I feel scared saying this, but I remember leaving early because you didn't feel well," she added.

"Right! That was the reason we ended class early," I agreed.

"Wow, I can barely believe I got through this," Doris explained.

"Tell me more about the challenge of this conversation," I suggested.

"I didn't know what I would do if you said I was wrong, insisting that we went home early because of the snow," she offered, with relief.

"What would you have done if I told you that you were wrong?"

"I would have felt awful. I mean after all, you're the teacher. I wouldn't have argued the point, and I would have walked away feeling defeated and helpless."

"That sounds awful! I guess you're saying that we would have been caught in a right-wrong dynamic and you would have deferred to me as the authority figure and gone away feeling very dissatisfied," I answered.

"What else could I have done?" she asked, her bewilderment palpable.

"What about asking me if I would be willing to create space for each of us to have a different memory and for no one to be right or wrong."

"I like that. But what if you said no and simply concluded that I was wrong and that was that?"

"One option is that you could have described the impact my position was having on you," I suggested.

"What would that have sounded like?"

"You might say, 'Sounds like you're telling me there's no room for different views in this conversation.'"

"What happens next?" Doris wondered.

"Well, if you hear that I'm attached to being right and unwilling to accommodate a different view, then you might consider whether I'm actually a viable resource for learning, creating, and exploring," I suggested.

Doris left our conversation seemingly appreciative of the opportunity to invite someone in the future to step away from being entrenched in a right-wrong dynamic and to soften into a receptivity to diverse thinking.

Other expressions of fighting include sarcasm, blaming, bullying, threatening, deception, and the much more subtle form: passive aggression. *Passive aggression* is anger expressed passively in the form of broken agreements, lateness, and forgetting, all done unconsciously and all having an unfavorable impact upon the recipient.

Vengeance is one of the more toxic expressions of fighting. It typically closes off our hearts in an attempt to avoid feeling hurt and/ or helpless. We cling to the illusion that we are entitled to hurt others, oblivious to the damage we inflict upon our own hearts in the process. Revenge prohibits us from receiving and learning about the inevitable enchantment that comes to a broken heart. So much is lost when we're trapped in a web of efforts to dominate. We lose the enchantment of welcome, inclusion, co-creation, collaboration, and learning from one another's uniqueness.

When fighting becomes a primary way of feeling safe, we begin to wrestle with life. In such a posture, there is no peace. We push and drive our wills toward the satisfaction of some desire or goal. Life is reduced to either a set of helpful events or unfortunate impediments. This combative focus takes us out of an intimate relationship with life.

We cannot witness life as a gift, as informing us more deeply about the journey and us, its pilgrims. The desire to seek is forfeited, and the price is disenchantment.

Fleeing

Flight is a natural reaction to danger, governed by the sympathetic adrenal system. When we are in situations that do not accommodate fleeing, the need to flee can also get frozen in our nervous system. The next step is to typically create stories about people, places and situations that keep us in avoidance. Narratives created from trapped flight energy heighten the likelihood of disenchantment. We live from: "I'm not going to be here." Our stories diminish our capacity for a full sensory experience, limiting our contact with the sublime. It also cuts us off from being touched, moved, supported, and loved by others.

The more we live in our flight stories, the more credibility we attribute to them. We behaviorally move away from perceived danger, we create a story supporting the alleged cogency of the perceived danger, and we likely feel both scared and unsafe. Our flight stories can run the gamut, describing the so-called perpetrator as evil, dangerous, mentally ill, untrustworthy, and malicious. Once we feel unsafe, it can be very difficult to generate a reasonable account of what or whom we define as dangerous.

Introverts run more of a risk of engaging in flight. By definition, they pull their energy in and away in order to process their beliefs and feelings. Hence, it takes very little to slip into severe distancing. While on the run, all the losses experienced through fighting occur, vaulting us into disenchantment.

When flight becomes second nature, we are running away from an intimate relationship with life. However, when we flee from life, we inevitably flee from ourselves, and any possibility of experiencing enchantment. We cut off the vital means of relating to life in the hope that life won't get us. We stop loving, dreaming, longing, needing, and desiring. These dynamic energies are sacrificed in the hope of not being disruptive, avoiding conflict, and protecting ourselves from disappointment.

Moving Out of Trapped Fight and Flight Energy

> *His safety depends on remaining present by employing the felt sense. In this way his finely tuned senses can pick up the slightest sound or movement. Internally, he may be warned of danger by an intangible sense that something isn't quite right. Smells are rich, colors bright and vibrant. Everything is bursting with life. In this state of awareness it is possible to find beauty in what otherwise might be perceived as mundane—a twig, a caterpillar, a drop of dew on a leaf.*
> —Peter Levine, *Waking the Tiger*

The key to moving out of disenchantment is to give our bodies permission to go through fighting and fleeing movements. We can punch, kick, yell and make aggressive gestures in a safe way. If we slow the movements down, the nervous system can more easily recalibrate, releasing the trapped fight and flight energy.

Pausing and calming happen by learning to ground. Grounding happens by doing any of the following: taking the breath to our center of gravity (one inch below the navel); feeling our feet firmly on the floor; loosening the jaw; tracking internal sensations (twitching, tightening, trembling, relaxation); and attending to external sensations of sight, smell, hearing, and touch. Calming the body down allows for greater mindfulness, which can help us be more discerning about what will actually provide real protection and how much protection we need, opening us to more vitality.

Pausing and calming gradually allow us to feel, name, and speak about our emotions. As we become less reactionary, learning to feel scared *and* safe, we can generate more options and, most importantly, begin to build an authentic support system. When we have such support, we have a place to feel vulnerable, we have a place to be seen and heard, we have a place to feel accepted and loved, and we have a place to explore ways of responding to life's challenges. Essentially, we create the kind of safety we needed right from birth: authentic attachment.

The single most important gain from being able to pause and calm ourselves is this ability to feel scared *and* safe. Safety begins to evolve as we become comfortable employing effective boundaries. Once we trust that we will say no to whatever feels unacceptable, intrusive, or abusive, we can begin to feel our fear and feel safe. Good boundaries are also reflected by a resolve to support our goodness and uniqueness in the presence of others having unfavorable reactions to our choices and beliefs.

Jennifer, a forty-five-year-old dental assistant, described to me her delight in travel.

"I've started traveling more alone, and I actually start crying when the plane begins to land back home," she explained.

"The travel is relatively new for you after having raised three children," I suggested.

"Yes, I just started traveling in the past year and really enjoy doing it alone."

"Do you have any hunch about what makes traveling alone so rewarding?" I asked.

"No, I don't. But I really love it."

"I have heard you describe your adult life as mostly about being dedicated to meeting the needs and expectations of others. However, lately, you seem to be more ready to prioritize your own needs."

"Yes, that's true, and it's much easier for me to do that when I'm alone," she pointed out.

"What makes it easier when you're alone?"

"I'm not sure. It's just much easier," she said.

"Well, I'm wondering if it might be much easier because you have a good physical boundary working for you, separating you from the expectations of others," I offered.

"I think that's it. I feel so much freer!" she exclaimed.

"I can appreciate this new level of freedom you're experiencing. But it's worth noting that your freedom seems to diminish significantly in the presence of others," I explained.

"What would I have to do in order to feel similar when interacting with others?" she asked.

"You would need to be willing to learn to pause, ground yourself in the presence of other folks, remain self-focused, and prepare to say yes or no to what's coming at you—and also develop enough resolve to tolerate others' having an unfavorable response to your wishes and ideas," I explained.

"Are you telling me that in flying, I have been employing physical boundaries in lieu of these other kinds of boundaries?"

"Exactly! Interacting with others calls for emotional boundaries that allow you to be yourself while engaging folks."

Jennifer was willing to learn about the kind of boundaries that would support her while in the presence of others, something she had never done. She was worried about returning to the old way of allowing herself to be taken hostage by the expectations of others and excited about the possibility of experiencing her relationships as a place where she could safely be herself.

Freezing

> *We've pretended too much in our family, Luke, and*
> *hidden far too much. I think we're all going to pay a high*
> *price for our inability to face the truth.*
> —Pat Conroy, *The Prince of Tides*

There are two prerequisites to getting injured or traumatized: you must have a body and something or someone is moving toward you with the potential of violating your boundaries. As fighting declares, "You're not going to be here," and flight declares, "My body is not going to be here," freeze says, "I'm not going to be here."

The psyche is well equipped to remove our life force from our bodies when facing overwhelming danger. Similar to the members of Conroy's family, when facing danger, we go into hiding. Movement is identified as dangerous; therefore, energies like feelings and desires that lead to motion are frozen. The process of dissociation siphons these energies out of the body, and we may have a blank look, almost trancelike.

From the dissociated freeze posture, life is an endless merry-go-round of disenchantment. The senses no longer take in the hues, tones, and timbre of our surroundings. At best, we create some interesting ideas about our experience. At its extreme, we begin replacing the vibrancy of a bodily experience with magical thoughts that disengage us from our surroundings. We no longer face the truth of what lives in our bodies and how it is informing us about our surroundings.

Melting the Freeze

Unlike fight and flight, which attempt to create safety for the body, freeze pretends we don't have a body. When we lock into freeze, we need to seek a healer who knows how to provide safety and welcome. We need help to slowly reclaim our bodies by first becoming more aware of our physical paralysis and then shifting gently to both internal and external mobility. As we welcome ourselves back to our bodies, we can feel vibrations of heat and tingling sensations. The initial key may be to move toes, ankles, gentle swaying, giving our eyes permission to look where they want to look with us following their lead, letting go of an intention that directs our gaze. The challenge will be to very gradually become comfortable with bodily energies of fight and flight.

The hope is that the more delicate and subtle sensations morph into larger expressions of sound and movements that are not threatening. As melting occurs, we experience the movement from being disembodied to somatic delight. We can define this as fledging enchantment, heading toward more feeling, more desire, and more heart. Hearts come to know love as we are moved by love's power. The forces of giving and receiving reclaim their fire, animating a capacity for passionate engagement.

Helpful Movements

> *Consciousness is only possible through change; change is only possible through movement.*
> —Aldous Huxley, *The Art of Seeing*

Having a body able to move safely and in accord with life's rhythms is a prerequisite to a life of enchantment. Melting the freeze is like awakening from the dead. Slowly, the freeze loses its rigidity, with the body beginning to claim its power to move back into the rhythm of life's changes.

Thanks to advances in neuroscience, we know now that there are many more neuron-transmitters from the body to the brain. For example, we know that the vagus nerve transmits impulses from the gut to the brain. Hence, Huxley is correct in suggesting through association that consciousness is only possible through movement.

The buds of enchantment begin with the body reclaiming the capacity to move. A number of gentle movements can be helpful. Sit on an exercise ball, balancing yourself as you sway back and forth. Tai Chi is a wonderful form of meditative movement. Some forms of circle dancing can be a part of reclaiming movement. I highly recommend a massage technique called Trager, which gently rocks limbs, joints, and muscle tissue.

Another great exercise is to sit in a chair with a straight back and a thick, soft pillow under your feet. Move your legs in a running motion, varying the pace, with your feet hitting the pillow. It's a wonderful way to allow your body to reclaim its entitlement for flight. The therapeutic model called Somatic Experiencing can also be extremely helpful in melting the freeze.

Enchantment

The spirit of enchantment is set free to unite with the world once it has safely united with the body. The body becomes melodically animated and aroused, called to some renewal of spirit. An old meaning of the word *enchantment* is "spellbound." We can understand enchantment as the condition of being under a spell, being enthusiastically animated by our experience. As we have seen, we must feel safe enough to feel arousal in our bodies. The more we are able to pause and ground ourselves, the more resilient we are, able to feel deep bodily arousal without acting in some injurious fashion.

Enchantment is typically accompanied by the temptation to unite with the source of the spell. It may be a person, a place, a thing, or an event that calls to us. I recall walking back to my fraternity after class one day and noticing sheets and peace signs hanging out the window of the executive office of the university president. As I got closer, it became obvious that a group of students had taken over the building in protest of the Vietnam War.

There was something magical about the entire event. I decided to pause and listen to the various speeches and music being played from a building typically bearing more refinement. Suddenly, a clergyman whom I respected called to me from the second-story window. He gestured to me to enter the building and join the protest. I froze in a

state of deep ambivalence. I believed in him and in the cause. I just
didn't know if I wanted to enter the building in order to demonstrate
my beliefs. I finally walked away, feeling as if I had let the clergyman
down.

I will always remember the great temptation to walk into that
building. Bringing discernment to temptation is important. Some
temptation calls us to ourselves while other temptation calls us away
from ourselves. To this day, I'm not sure what temptation I followed
that day outside the president's office—whether I was tempted to
move toward or away from myself. We can ask, Does this temptation
harm me or others? Is this temptation held in compassion? Is this
temptation compatible with my values? Does this temptation support
what is sustainable?

With all enchantment there is a letting go and a willingness to be
touched and moved by someone or something outside of ourselves.
There can be both the feeling of being out of control and the feeling
of being connected to something larger than ourselves. Falling in love
is a classic example, the verb *fall* denoting a loss of control leading
to a larger experience. Seekers must be willing to fall into their
pilgrimage, allowing their experience to inform them. The magic of
this falling weaves an enchantment that is about unity, and unity is
about intimacy. Living an enchanted life means living intimately.

The Intimate Life

Living intimately is not popular. It carries that loss of control
suggested by the word *fall*, as in falling in love. The ego protests the
locus of control being removed from it. It also means feeling a wide
range of physical sensations and emotional energies. It often means
being willing to feel vulnerable, which happens when someone or
some event has the power to create a variety of different feelings
in us, including hurt. We can understand this receptivity to being

emotionally impacted as *sensitivity*, which we will explore in this section along with four other characteristics of the intimate life: sweetness, living in a meaningful story, renewing a faith in life, and learning to consecrate our experience.

Sensitivity

Many folks have come to my counseling practice discouraged and/ or ashamed about their sensitivity. They are convinced that the gods have conspired against them, doling out a serious defect of character.

We live in a culture considerably confused about the power of sensitivity. At best, we're told it's a quality fitting for children and a liability for adults, especially men. We will need to lean against cultural influences in order to reclaim the power of sensitivity.

One of the strengths afforded us by sensitivity is empathy. My old friend and colleague Henri Nouwen often wrote in praise of the empathic encounter, saying "Simply being with someone is difficult because it asks of us that we share in the other's vulnerability, enter with him or her into the experience of weakness and powerlessness, become part of the uncertainty, and give up control and self-determination."

The capacity for empathic resonance calls us to the defeats, losses, and vulnerabilities of others. Empathy allows us to live into the suffering of the other, creating a salient unity. We let go of the ego's fascination with offering advice and solutions.

Sensitivity only becomes a liability if we either get hooked by heroic aspirations or become naive about how our sensitivity might be received by others. Stepping into a hero's posture is easily driven by attempts to save, rescue, or fix others. Sensitivity loses its potency when we dishonor our limits. It also becomes a liability when we assume the world will automatically be considerate and gentle with our sensitivity.

Having good emotional boundaries becomes a critical way to carry our sensitivity. We can be empathic with the suffering of others, reminding ourselves that it is not our suffering. Allowing for empathic resonance with good boundaries allows the seeker to learn from relationships without being completely exhausted by endless attempts to control the uncontrollable.

When we release a naïveté about how people might respond to our sensitivity, we can carry our heart with a readiness to protect it when necessary. We do not allow ourselves to bring tenderness where it may be abused or exploited. We live with an open heart but prepared to employ a boundary where needed. The key is to trust that we will maintain an empathy that allows us to change and learn wherever possible *and* protect the heart that generates that empathy. As Carl Rogers puts it, "Over the years . . . the research evidence keeps piling up, and it points strongly to the conclusion that a high degree of empathy in a relationship is possibly the most potent and certainly one of the most potent factors in bringing about change and learning." Empathic resonance opens us to diverse experience and new ways of feeling, thinking, and acting.

I was complaining to my old friend Pete about the loss of meaning around the holidays, especially Christmas. Pete is fifteen years older than I, and I regularly benefit from his years. He told the following story in response to my holiday disillusionment.

> I also spent some time complaining about the superficiality of Christmas. Then, some twenty years ago, while leaving church one day, I overheard Pastor English talking to some parishioners about families who were struggling. I went home and began to wonder why I didn't realize that some folks were significantly financially challenged. I made an appointment with Pastor English and listened to the stories of families who needed the bare essentials, food and clothing. I realized how far removed I had been from reality.

I began to access a renewed empathy for folks less fortu-nate than myself. During the next several years, the pastor identified for me several families in need. I would give the pastor a check to cover food, clothes, and gifts for the children. I decided to make this offering anonymously. I learned how much I had been attached to being recognized for the giving I did throughout my entire life. I was learning to give with no strings.

One family had a son in middle school named Josh. I often saw him around the playground. He struck me as being a loner. I joined Big Brothers, and they connected me with Josh. At first, he didn't say much. We went to ballgames, the movies, and fishing. As he moved into adolescence, he opened up more, talking about his challenges at home and at school. I was learning to listen in a new way, giving less advice and fewer recommendations. I liked it.

Well, Josh went to the community college and starting talking about a vocation as a Unitarian minister, but his family could not afford to send him to seminary. I made an appointment with Pastor English to hear what he thought about Josh being called to seminary. He said he thought Josh was a natural, a sure fit for the ministry, and that it was unfortunate that his family could not financially swing it.

I suggested that I was in a position to support Josh's attendance at seminary. The pastor immediately began blessing my generosity. I reminded him that I would do it for Josh and me and that I wanted it to be anonymous. The pastor objected, pointing out that such a large offering needed to be acknowledged. I told him that's exactly why it must be anonymous— and anyway, after all those years, I wasn't sure what being acknowledged for my giving would even feel like. Last month I went to Josh's first service. He's one hell of a minister.

My old friend had stepped into empathy and changed his entire life. Pete remains one of the greatest listeners I've ever been graced to be in the presence of.

Sensitivity remains a source of power when we grow a resiliency to the bumps and dangers along the way. It is only too easy to feel overly victimized or to get sanctimonious as a way to puff ourselves up, away from the sting of hurt. Becoming vindictive attempts to move us out of the feeling of helplessness that accompanies feeling hurt. Revenge lifts us into some cursory feeling of potency as we prepare to inflict pain on others.

Sensitivity operates as a great gift when we are able to keep our heart open while protecting it. It will not be helpful to naïvely believe that everyone will treat us kindly because we show up with a big heart. My old mentor George tells the story of a man willing to live with an open heart and do what is necessary to protect it.

A colleague approached him at a Christmas party and sarcastically commented, "George, I do believe you are one of the most sensitive men in our group."

George responded, "If you insist upon talking about my sensitivity sarcastically, you'll find out that I can also be one of the meanest sons of bitches in our group."

George remains a great inspiration to me regarding living with an immense heart without allowing others to exploit and abuse it.

Seekers can carry their sensitivity as a great gift if they remain empathic, trusting that they will protect themselves from being unnecessarily vulnerable. A largeness of heart keeps them living intimately.

Sweetness

> *Behave so the aroma of your actions may enhance the general sweetness of the atmosphere.*
>   —Henry David Thoreau

There is a softness about sweetness. Whether it is due to the way we act or talk, our expression is received as sweet when it lands gently. We move in a way that is engaging but not intrusive. Our voices are audible but not piercing. We make requests rather than demands. We have hunches rather than well-constructed and well-articulated positions. We offer eye contact that is inviting and not challenging. We value comfort over challenge and competition. We remain sensitive to what lands softly on the senses, the heart, and the mind.

Sweetness happens as we remember and re-member the lives of others. We remember as we bring to mind some unique aspect of another's preferences and sentiments. We *re-member* when we actually bring some member or element of their lives that touches and moves them, moving out of a mental state into action, adding to what is practical and uneventful. An ordinary day is re-membered as we make an offering of a person's favorite flowers or music, an invitation to a preferred event, or the preparation of a desired dish.

We can also re-member an environment by bringing more light, soft resonance, plant life, and color, as well as artifacts that touch our hearts. We re-member our surroundings by touching the environment with what touches us.

African-American women who were hired domestic help raised my wife in the South. These women were devotionally her surrogate parents, as depicted in the film *The Help*. Photographs of these women in our home present images evoking a generosity of heart that palpably cuts across racial barriers. These photos of women who loved and nurtured a little white girl soften and calm tensions caused by ignorance and fear in people who visit us. Our home is re-membered by the sweetness captured by these photographs, especially as they kindle fond memories of my wife's childhood. These images also offer a sweet holding of the extremes of racial unrest in the South and the heartfelt care given to a white child by African-American women.

Recently, I had been struggling a bit. I awoke one morning to see a dozen orange tulips on my nightstand. I don't see myself as a flower guy and yet found the bouquet regularly drawing my attention. Like most men, I have attributed sweetness as a need of the opposite gender. However, these tulips demanded I notice their sweetness. They reflected my wife's large heart, her sensitivity and compassion for my stumblings. I allowed myself to be wrapped in the softness of her sweetness.

Sweetness often happens when we hear certain words. It can be a poem, lyrics to a song, a prayer, or a chant. There is a chant that opens my chest and heart. When I recite it, my body seems to understand the words, although my mind ascribes no meaning to the lines. The following is the chant that brings me great sweetness:

> Ma Durga
> Jaya Jagatambe
> Jai Jaya Jagatambe
> Hey Ma Durga
> Hey Ma Durga

A growing capacity for acceptance is an enchanting expression of sweetness. An old definition of the word *acceptance* is "to receive willingly." Receiving life's offerings that lie outside of our control supports intimate living. We can gradually put protest, blame, and victimization to rest. Acceptance refuses to turn against life. To all things out of our control, acceptance announces an abiding willingness to receive life on life's terms.

There is a softness about acceptance that opens to healing and learning while facing adversity. We can pause and ask, What will help me to accept this adversity lying outside my control? What is this trouble asking of me? What resources are available to help me identify life's request? What depth of emotion do I need to feel in order to open to life's request? What allies do I have to help me stay the course, holding the sacredness of this trial?

There is also an immense sweetness in wildness, heartfelt wildness. It can be difficult to see the sweetness of wildness because of the danger often accompanying it. This wildness can be seen in Christ's disruption of the money changers in the temple. We see it in Gandhi's passive resistance, standing right at the edge of reacting violently to British rule. It shows up in Martin Luther King's crossing the Edmund Pettus Bridge on the way to Selma. It is displayed in Mandela's appointing to his cabinet the man who beat him in the prison yard. In each of these cases, the sweetness of wildness cast off what was appropriate and acceptable in order to make room for more heart.

Seekers need to live with such wildness so they can respond to their heart's calling. What is the larger sin: to live with wildness of heart, risking causing harm; or to remain at a great distance from our hearts, taking asylum within the house of public opinion?

When we fear the danger that lives close to wildness, we run the risk of retreating to the high ground of morality and self-righteousness. We replace the truth of our fear of danger with a high-minded posture insulating us from a full heart. Striving toward being virtuous separates us from life. While hiding behind the pillars of purity, we deny the profound urges of the heart.

Urges of the heart often carry a measure of darkness, which includes resentment, possessiveness, jealousy, vindictiveness, and cruelty. Once we have created a solid kinship with self-righteousness, we begin flying under the radar, striving to present a pristine image. The virtuous eagerly demonstrate how compatible their actions are with prevailing norms, no matter how incompatible they are with some inner darkness. The battle between the psyche and these darker energies typically leads to depression or much anxiety—both of which interrupt any intimacy with life.

When we present ourselves as manifestations of essential goodness, we must separate from those who reveal some darkness within us, even if it means leaving our own soul in exile. The sweetness of forgiveness, welcome, and inclusion is lost. Sweetness is replaced by the bitterness of separation, ridicule, and condemnation.

In his essay "A Chapter on Ears," Charles Lamb unfavorably compares certain types of music to several things, including "To pile honey upon sugar, and sugar upon honey, to an interminable, tedious sweetness." Authentic sweetness is a delicious invitation to life. It supports intimate living. However, excessive or inauthentic sweetness places something darker or bitter in hiding. For example, a number of years ago, my friend Charles described dating a woman and what it was like to discover someone piling honey upon sugar and sugar upon honey.

> I had been dating Maureen for several months. One Friday evening we were hanging out at my favorite coffee shop, where they were playing live music. During the evening some dozen or so folks approached our table to say hello. I began to notice that Maureen was offering everyone who approached us a copious number of compliments. I asked Maureen if she were very familiar with everyone she greeted. She said she knew two or three of them. She was handing out accolades like door prizes, to people she hardly knew! The more we saw one another, the more I could see that

she was highly conflict avoidant. I began to wonder if underneath the sweetness of all those compliments, some covert deal was being made regarding how she wanted to be approached—that is, to be engaged only with appropriate pleasantries.

Living in a Meaningful Story

But with awareness that one's life is grounded in eternal stories and motifs, one's own personal story begins to feel enchanted, and this feeling gives rise to a love of one's own life that is the cure for narcissism, insecurity, and self-doubt.

—Thomas Moore, *The Re-Enchantment of Everyday Life*

In an ongoing way, we are all living in some story. The major themes in our stories may be about ambition, loss, success, defeat, or last night's ball scores. However, meaningful and intimate stories reflect enduring themes, themes that transcend time and place.

The enduring nature of our stories opens us to a love affair with our own lives as we shed some petty attachment lacking soul. One of these eternal themes that is a cure for narcissism is a devotion to service. The theme of service is reflected in numerous old stories, like the story of Moses, the Arthurian knights, and Ghandhi. Again, the two fundamental energies of intimacy are giving and receiving. When we are in service, we are giving to life. We are meaningfully participating in our lives, moving beyond simply meeting our personal needs. Our giving creates rapport with life.

We can ask, What service is calling to me? What lifestyle adjustments may need to happen in order to step into this service?

What fears might inhibit me from offering this service? What allies do I have that can help me assess my readiness to offer this service?

It's only too easy to inflate the nature of an honorable service, diminishing anything falling short of a two-year stint in the Peace Corps. We can say that we are serving a person, a group, or an event when we fervently ask what the person or event is asking for. What might bring more healing, more peace, more care, more comfort, more insight, and more creativity are the kinds of curiosities guiding how we might serve.

There can be substantial simplicity in our offerings. For example, while recently attending a conference, a man noticed me sitting with my left foot housed in a surgical boot and asked if he could get me a tea. Holding the faith that our lives are about remaining in service to life keeps us in a meaningful story.

Renewing a Faith in Life

As Moore points out, a love of one's own life is a cure for insecurity. When we live from insecurity, we are more retiring and yielding. We step away from life. We can view insecurity as a loss of faith and trust in life. When we hold an abiding faith in life, we lean heartfully into the lived experience. However, it is critical to ask, what does it look like to believe in life? There are at least four essential elements to maintaining faith in life: refusing to remain a victim of life, accepting the life task of taking risks, learning to make mistakes, and devotionally remaining a student of life. We look at each of these elements in detail below.

Refusing to Remain a Victim of Life

If we define ourselves as victims of life, we automatically define life as an evil perpetrator. Obviously, the depraved and corrupt do not deserve our trust and faith. It is easy to move into being a victim when we feel hurt and helpless. The key here is to feel hurt and accept being powerless, so we do not have to turn against life. Remaining in an intimate relationship with life is similar to remaining in any relationship. We need to learn to feel hurt and helpless and remain curious about what our experience is asking us to learn or what risk it is asking us to take.

The more we can release idyllic visions of what life should be like, the more likely we are to live life on life's terms and not on our own terms. When life is actually the beloved, we yearn to understand it, accept it, and remain open to what it is asking for. We gradually give up juvenile protests of what brings us hurt, displeasure, and disappointment. The more we accept life for what it is rather than demanding it be the way we wish it to be, the easier it is to hold faith in life with an open heart.

Accept the Life Task of Taking Risks

If we can accept that life is essentially mysterious, insecure, and unpredictable, then we might be able to accept the appropriateness of taking risks on such a journey. It will be mostly about committing to our healing, allowing us to move beyond rigidly employing fighting, fleeing, and freezing as ways to be alive. Once we are able to avoid being overwhelmed by bodily sensations and emotions, we can find safety in employing effective boundaries and securing viable support from others.

We do not fear taking risks. Taking risks is not mostly an issue of available courage; what we actually fear is how we will treat ourselves when the risks we take yield unfavorable consequences. Hence, the strongest form of safety we can provide ourselves is self-forgiveness when facing the discouraging results of having taken a risk.

Learning to Make Mistakes

Making mistakes often suggests failing to employ knowledge we possess or operating with inadequate information. Given life's immensity, we will not get life right. Any serious attempt to avoid making mistakes has us avoiding life. Being intimate with life is seriously maligned when we demand that we live a mistake-free life. Self-forgiveness again becomes a critical offering as we make mistakes, resisting turning against ourselves or against life. Our capacity to forgive ourselves goes a long way toward supporting our faith in life.

Devotionally Remaining a Student of Life

Our love of and faith in life are supported as we remain devotionally receptive to life's teachings. Remaining a student of life sustains the meaning of our relationship with life. We are not simply having a good time or trying to be happy or successful. Rather, learning remains our priority. We can hold the faith that life will present a bounty of opportunity for instruction.

Even when we move into bad faith or resist believing in life, we can describe it as our loss of faith in life rather than building a case that life is undeserving of anyone's faith. We can see our lived experiences as similar to breakdowns in any love relationship. We lose faith, we lose trust, we lose resiliency—and hopefully, we learn to make our way back to an intimate connection.

The Commitment to Consecrate

> *On the death of a friend, we should consider that the fates through confidence have devolved on us the task*

of a double living, that we have henceforth to fulfill the
promise of our friend's life also, in our own, to the world.
　　　　　　　　　　　—Henry David Thoreau

Thoreau reminds us of an abiding intimacy we can have with life as we support a friend's promise to life as well as our own. We might support our dead friend's family or some professional project or cause he or she was devoted to. Our promise can be seen as our nuptial vow to life: to honor, love, and serve. We can see this promise as *the commitment to consecrate.*

When we are willing to consecrate what presents itself, we are actively bringing sacredness to our lives. An old meaning of the word *sacred* is "to sacrifice." Because life is essentially about change and loss, we consecrate our lives by devotionally learning how to endure loss and whatever is being sacrificed in our losses.

We consecrate our lives by earnestly living questions regarding what deserves our reverence. We then commit to pausing in acknowledgement and honoring moments of reverence. We can do this by our silent presence or by some verbal recognition, prayer, or the enactment of a ritual.

We remain intimately connected to life as we define ourselves as the consecrators, those willing to make life sacred. This will call for a large vision if we hope to avoid becoming self-righteousness. Consecrators must commit to doing their best to live from truth, compassion, and forgiveness. If they fail to do so, they simply bestow sanctification upon what is in the service of their egos. There is great magic as we allow ourselves to see both the darkness and the light with consecrating eyes.

A Blessing for Enchantment

Magic asks us to remember our creatureliness. Learning to release our grip upon winning and being right, pausing and feeling the waves of energy in our animal body, begins to free our senses, allowing them to welcome the beautiful. We come to see that our body was always longing to feel safe enough to live intimately.

There will be enchantment once we awaken the body to its natural animation. We must come back to this body—its twitching, contracting, expanding, softening, becoming heavier with variances of warmth. Ready to feel the body's subtle nature, we move to the larger emotional energies: fear, sadness, anger, and joy. The stage is set for the delight of enchantment.

No longer defining domination as the way to be safe or allowing our voices to drop away into the vacuum of a consuming yielding, we no longer need to flee the moment with no recourse. We have become students of this thing called present time. We are more deeply prepared to be touched, moved, and informed by our experience.

As we find comfort in our relationship with the ground, safe now to open to enchantment, we pause, asking the breath to take us to that place where our feet know their belonging to the earth. Now the magic can find us, no longer trapped in an ever-rising swirl of energy.

We now begin to live intimately in rhythm with the sublime. Life hears our voices in a heartfelt petition. We want to know life and be touched by life. A new resonance lives in our bodies, one acquainted with the fire of our own wills and the grace needed to surrender to the will of life.

Sensitivity stops being an impediment and is now an opening to ever-deepening connections. No longer guided by innocence, our heart knows where a welcome awaits this opening. We feel more, we are more, and so life brings us more. Sweetness replaces the bitterness that accompanied either fighting with life or running from it.

We live now as seekers in a meaningful story. Our souls know a new peace. We know our Place. We have come to learn and to serve. We will forget our spiritual errand and will need to find a place for pause and remembering we come here to consecrate, to make sacred even that which remains deeply mysterious.

7

The Aging Seeker

We may either continue in our last years to cling to our past achievements and worn-out values, thus sinking eventually into complete dependence on others, on collective opinions, demands, and attitudes; or we may confront our growing weakness and loss of energy . . . and so approach that kind of free dependence on "the other" which brings us to the meaning of forgiveness and to kinship with all things.

—Helen M. Luke

IN THE ABOVE QUOTE, LUKE suggests that aging may offer us the opportunity to "be brought to the meaning of forgiveness and to kinship with all things." We can say that unity or kinship with all things is at the heart of mysticism. It may be that the purpose of the aging seeker is to move toward a kinship with all things. Could it be that this kinship Luke refers to is another definition of *home* for the seeker? Might it be that a separation from youth actually prompts a kind of initiation into a kinship with all things?

Coming to know this kinship will call for great mindfulness and great heart. It will mean being willing to remain in a deeply intimate relationship with life. This life connection can only be woven by a refusal to see our suffering as simply a condemnation to being victims of life. It will be important to settle into the question, what is this suffering asking for? It will also call for a gradual dethroning of the ego's alleged dominion over life. This conquer-or-be-conquered attitude will need to give way to a sustained connection to life. We cannot effectively learn by staying at war with life. It will mean calling off hostilities and finding the resolve to weather a myriad of unplesantries and defeats. Without this armistice and willingness to generate a creative rapport with life, we run the risk of experiencing aging as simply the acquisition of years, leading to little or no deepening.

Michael Meade explores this in his discussion of elderhood:

> This can be seen as the problem of the olders vs. the elders. Traditionally, elders carry a greater vision of life because they develop insight into their own lives. The elders are those who found threads of purpose and meaning amidst the illusions and delusions of life. Amidst the inevitable troubles of life, the bubble of the "closed ego" bursts and a deeper, wiser self is born. Such psychological maturity involves a shift from a self-centered life to one of genuine meaning and of greater service to others.

We don't start becoming elders when we are old. Elderhood is the result of years of being a seeker. I have worked with numerous young men and women who have begun paving a path to elderhood; I often can see the face of a much older person in the recesses of their glowing youthful cheeks. They are seekers allowing their experiences of loss, addiction, and rejection to forge a curiosity about how to creatively dance with the perilous journey of life. They are restless, their restlessness vaulting them beyond the grips of mediocrity. Their souls possess an urgency pushing them beyond convention. They long for someone to hear the stories of their sufferings and help them give this suffering meaning that will allow for a sustained intimacy with their lived experience. They are willing to entertain what might need to be sacrificed in order to engender more meaning.

Inevitably, they experience a level of dis-illusionment (I spell the word *disillusionment* this way to denote undoing illusion) as some myth that offered guidance to their early years begins to crumble. It may be that *olders*, as opposed to *elders*, have not effectively experienced such dis-illusionment, keeping them captive to the worn-out values and fears Luke warns us of.

M. Scott Peck addresses the emotional inertia indicative of olders in his book *The Different Drum*:

> Most, to a greater or lesser degree, fail to individuate— to separate—ourselves from family, tribe, or caste. Even into old age we remain figuratively tied to the apron strings of our parents and culture. We are still dictated to by the values and expectations of our mothers and fathers. We still follow the direction of the prevailing wind and bow before the shibboleths of our society. We go with the crowd. From laziness and fear—fear of loneliness, fear of responsibility, and other nameless dreads—we never truly learn to think for ourselves or dare to be out of step with the stereotypes.

When we "follow the direction of the prevailing wind," we don't allow ourselves to be dis-illusioned. In this chapter, let's explore some of the great myths of youth that need to die at the hands of dis-illusionment in order for an elder to be born.

Magnificent Myths of Youth

It is important for youth to attach themselves to myths that typically require a level of self-aggrandizement. When young people are not properly initiated into the mysteries of life, they attribute a wide range of competencies and skills to themselves in order to create a bravado, allowing them to face life with idealism, hope, and self-trust. They have not been told that their best efforts to understand their experience will not penetrate the mystery of life. There is no grasp of rightsizing their egos; hence, they run with the most expansive ego possible.

The formation of a strong ego is important to our development. Under another title, I have described the benefits of a solid ego, which include the following: being able to identify what we want, the ability to formulate an intention to manifest desire, feeling entitled to receive good things, the ability to generate our own values and make choices reflective of those values, and the ability to employ boundaries for protection and safeguarding individual uniqueness. The dilemma is that the average ego is not satisfied with these competencies as it constructs a more grandiose vision of itself, attempting to cope with a lack of proper initiation.

Olders do not allow for enough dis-illusionment of the youthful myths in order to have the bubble of the closed ego burst open. Hence, wisdom is not available to them, as they remain in service to an ego preoccupied with impressing itself. Let's take a look at several of these magnificent myths of youth, which are aimed at giving homage to the ego and obstructing an emerging wisdom:

"I'm going to live forever."

A popular myth is the belief that we will be here for a very long time—maybe forever. As silly as it may sound, there's unformulated belief about one's immortality—*unformulated* meaning that it isn't thought about much and we act as if it were true. Hence, the future becomes the place to live in, to plan for, to prepare for, and to anticipate. Our anticipation of the future's glorious arrival nudges young people out of the moment, the only place where real personal power exists. Because we live in a death-denying culture, the illusion of permanence gets easily integrated into the fabric of the ego.

"It should be easy to decide what's right, what's true, and what deserves my attention."

Life is often reduced to a board game like Monopoly. Roll the dice and decide if you're ready to purchase Boardwalk. There is a very low tolerance for ambiguity. Self-doubt and feeling lost and confused are belittled as if there's something wrong with the person facing such quandaries. The illusion is that real adults do not lose their way. Ultimately, a heavy price is paid for clinging to the pretense of certainty.

James Hollis says, "The suppression of doubt is the secret seed of fanaticism in all its forms, and therefore the secret drive engine in bigotry, sexism, homophobia, fundamentalism, and all other forms of contrived certainties." What Hollis calls a contrived certainty tends to place serious restrictions upon our ability to access imagination, curiosity, and wonder. Those energies are critical for maintaining an intimate relationship with the mystery of life. We sacrifice a real connection to life in the name of allegedly securing the ego's grandeur, while employing a major obstruction to elderhood.

"All I really need is me."

A common myth of youth is generated by an obsession with self-reliance. Asking for help is reduced to a statement of weakness. This is especially true of young men. Proving we can do it ourselves leads us to unnecessary defeats, a reproduction of the familiar, and serious denial about our limits. When independence is given supreme authority, it becomes easy to slip into rationalization about our failures, generating a skewed self-concept poorly depicting who we really are.

This myth tends to generate some unfortunate fallout in relationships. There's confusion about how to present feelings of vulnerability and need to a friend or partner. When self-reliance is pushed, it fosters unnecessary levels of isolation. We cannot reach out to those who love us, and we cannot be reached by them. Nor can we face the creative tension of learning to solve problems, make mutually satisfying decisions, resolve conflict, give and receive love at a deep level, and champion the uniqueness of those whom we love as well as honor our own uniqueness.

"Life is about demonstrating how special I am."

Sustained service to the ego's sovereignty is expressed by an attachment to being special. The ego wants to shine and raise its banners in praise of its achievements and successes. However, being special typically involves hierarchy: someone is on top and someone is on the bottom. The dilemma is that being on top demands endless demonstrations of our entitlement to an exalted status. We become so enthralled with proving ourselves that we seriously hamper our learning about life and about ourselves. We lose insight into our own lives. We are busy confirming our personal worth, which is never truly ours since our focus is to document our worth, not hold it as simply real.

Vanity is a natural accompaniment to striving to be special. An old meaning of the word *vanity* is "empty." Vanity is empty of authentic self-love. Vanity is a big person's way of playing dress-up. We eagerly pursue the favor of others, hoping our hair remains properly coiffed with all the impressive accoutrements of attire, speech, and physical movement, which demonstrates some level of excellence and poise. Vanity leaves us at the mercy of others, hoping they notice and respond approvingly. The real price for vanity is that we can't be loved, since only our showpieces are on display; we are actually not present yet.

"My purpose is to know and control people, places, and things."

I call this the "I've come to take command of life" myth. The great sacrifice created by belief in this myth is the focus on and benefits of self-insight. Since we have more control over ourselves than anywhere else, we lose a tremendous amount of power when we focus on everything but ourselves.

Once confused about what we feel, value, and believe, we easily become caught in a web of reactionaryism. Now people, places, and things hold dominion over us, pushing us into varied reactions, thus controlling how we behave. The very outcome we were determined to prevent becomes real. All forms of external events have the power to take us hostage, defining who we are.

"It's important always to be happy."

It is extremely easy to allow this myth to stay with us way beyond its life expectancy. What appears to be about joy and lightness is actually quite tragic. First of all, like love, happiness cannot be pursued. Second, the imperative to be happy replaces the richer directive to be authentic, which easily moves us into pretending we are happy. Third, emotional states such as sadness, discouragement, and hopelessness define us as failures. Fourth, it becomes increasingly difficult to allow the more challenging feeling states to inform us regarding what we need, where we belong, and how we want to live. It may be that contentment or happiness ultimately depends upon something much greater than the ego. As Robert Johnson and Jerry Ruhl point out, "You cannot acquire contentment like some consumer item, but you can awaken to its gifts. It is closer to the truth to say that contentment comes to us by divine grace."

Dethroning the Ego

Dethroning—but not beheading—the ego best guides us into elderhood. As mentioned earlier, the ego can serve us and serve us well, especially if there's a willingness to reduce its swelling. It will likely take a good deal of loss, pain, and dis-illusionment before we pause, ask for help, and begin to wonder who we are and what is the nature of this journey we call life. Our chronological aging happens to us as the years mount up. However, our psychological aging can happen because of us, giving us some measure of control over our maturation.

As quoted earlier, Meade suggests that elders "found purpose and meaning amidst the illusions and delusions of life." It may not be perfectly clear how the finding of meaning and purpose happens for us when we are broken by the ferocity of life. But there may be some magic in the defeat; some measure of transformation may happen when we do not know how to overcome life's adversity. Embracing genuine powerlessness may be the most meaningful and effective way to escort the ego off the throne.

I was twenty-nine when life's forces began roaring, putting some real chinks in my heroic armor. My wife was pregnant, we had lost a child shortly after birth, and our two-year-old daughter was 100 percent disabled. I had followed all the appropriate social and academic scripts, and here I was facing loss, helplessness, and bewilderment. A good friend suggested I see a particular counselor whom he strongly recommended. After struggling with my compulsive self-reliance, I called and made an appointment.

It took several sessions before I loosened my grip on the attitude of "I don't really know why I'm here. After all, I'm twenty-nine, and it's not like I don't know what I'm doing." This was followed by several more sessions, in which I finally grasped that the person sitting in front of me truly wanted to know me and be helpful.

Joyce, my counselor, pointed out that given the challenges facing my family, I seemed to have no idea whether I wanted my wife to terminate the present pregnancy or carry this fetus to full term. She also suggested how helpless I must feel, given that the ultimate decision sat with my wife. She went on to describe me as quite angry, which did not fit my attachment to having it all together and looking good. After all, the astute philosophy professor that I was could not possibly be struggling with something so primitive as anger. However, it became increasingly obvious that a smoldering blaze burned within me.

A severely inflated ego placed me way beyond having genuine needs, with an alleged immunity to the need for real support. My heroic aspirations left me in a state of emotional deprivation and very angry about having abandoned my humanity. I was slowly discovering there was no meaningful replacement for simply being myself, and that left me with a gnawing emptiness.

I felt trapped and betrayed by life. I was left with the death of one daughter, the ever-growing responsibilities and demands of attending to a completely disabled child, and another child on the way. For the first time in my life, I had no interesting answers. I decided to follow Joyce's lead. I committed to being more conscious of my anger, feeling it and expressing it appropriately.

When I encountered anyone I had a good rapport with, I responded to "How are you?" with "I'm angry." I recall meeting with the president of the college where I taught philosophy. I met his inquiry regarding how things were going with "I'm very angry," which immediately generated his concern. I reassured him that I was not about to do anything stupid but that I was very committed to creating a more conscious relationship with my anger. I look back upon those days and can't help wondering if a helpful ego was possibly behind my budding devotion to living more mindfully.

I began to see how my denied anger easily translated into passive aggression, manifested by self-righteousness and a propensity to take the psychological inventory of those around me. Defining myself as an angry man helped nudge me away from much more lofty ways of seeing myself. However, some forty years later, I remain receptive to the seduction of some inflated version of myself. A shift for which I'm grateful is that there is some likelihood of noticing I am drifting toward a swollen self-perception.

Meade may be correct when he says about elders, "Traditionally, elders carry a greater vision of life because they develop insight into their own lives." What is the connection between self-insight and a greater vision of life? Is it possible that we get a greater relationship with life when the ego has a lesser relationship with itself?

The Self-Examining Seeker

> *I have been and still am a seeker, but I have ceased to question stars and books; I have begun to listen to the teaching my blood whispers to me.*
>
> —Hermann Hesse

There may be no better preparation for entering old age as an elder than listening to the teaching our blood whispers to us. One of the great gifts we give to others and to the process of chronologically aging is to have diminished disparity between our psychological age and our chronological age. The first step toward supporting our psychological age is to exercise some commitment to remain self-examining. If we refuse to take on such a commitment, we run the risk of remaining defined by the myths of youth, leaving us with distorted views of ourselves and of life.

What does it take to begin being authentically self-examining, self-aware, or mindful? What does it take to sustain a commitment to live in a self-examining fashion? How can a life of self-examination help dethrone the ego? Richard Rohr puts it this way: "To know the truth, you must become the truth." Rohr reminds us that the business of seeking the truth must be deeply personal. We can become the truth of our struggles to be more compassionate and more authentic, to act with more integrity, and to learn to carry failure. We become the truth by our devotion to these enduring ways of being. This is especially true of forgiveness. Becoming the truth of self-forgiveness brings grace to our quest for truth. Grace allows us to carry confusion with suppleness, not demanding that life reveal its mysteries to us. We are willing to delight in our curiosity and wonder, thankful for the opportunity to discover what lives in us and around us.

Four significant lessons deepen our understanding of what lives in us and around us: learning how to accept being powerless; learning how to gain meaning from suffering; learning how to be dependent, with emphasis upon learning how to receive; and deepening our capacity for compassion.

Powerlessness

Nothing gets the ego's attention more than being powerless and feeling it. But before that happens, we typically feel most comfortable simply denying we are powerless, regardless of the challenge. Being powerless is a heavy blow to the ego's favorite delusion that it can exercise command over life's most prodigious predicaments. It will inevitably take suffering some serious consequences in order to acknowledge that life may be bigger than us. If we refuse to develop a keen eye for distinguishing what is and what is not in our control, and if we do not find the humility to let go of what is not in our control, then we will not be able to deepen our psychological age.

Accepting that we are powerless when the facts of the situation say we are powerless teaches us who we are and what life is. So often, people come to my office suffering from guilt, shame, and deep feelings of inadequacy because they believe they should have had mastery over something or someone completely out of their control.

I hear things like the following: "If I'd had had a different conversation with him before he left, he wouldn't have gotten into the accident." "I know if I had only listened to him more attentively, he would not have returned to drinking." "If I had come home earlier from the office, she would not have had the affair." "If I had turned that report in on time, I never would have gotten laid off." "She may have made it through the night if I had not gotten caught in traffic." "If I had helped him more with his homework, he would have been at the head of his class."

We massage our insecurities by attributing illusions of power to ourselves. When we are able to gradually diminish the ego's grandiosity, we can begin to know the person we really are. Our limits offer us a realistic contour. We begin to understand where we begin and end. If we can see the advantages of knowing and accepting our limits, then we can bring more ease to remaining self-examining and stewarding our psychological aging.

There are also serious cultural impediments to embracing our powerlessness. For example, the publishing industry is aware of the resistance of the collective ego to accepting being powerless. Hence, it insists upon marketing titles suggesting that readers can easily come to terms with immense topics in several easy steps. Such titles might include these:

Eight Steps to a Perfect Marriage
Seven Strategies Guaranteeing Effective Leadership
Nine Steps to Complete Happiness
Three Steps to the Perfect Date
Five Steps to Reaching Full Actualization

And so on. One of these days, I expect to see the title *Three Ways to Avoid Dying*!

It may take numerous attempts at trying to control people, places, and things before we can experience a sensibility about what is actually in our control. It is helpful simply to live the question of what lies beyond our power, over and over again. The hope is that we discover that our own inner worlds constitute the place where our power is maximized. Our beliefs, feelings, and actions are what we have dominion over. With some support and luck, we may find ourselves increasingly interested in who we are. If that happens, self-examination has a chance to become a way of life, and as it does, we will have the good fortune of entering old age as an elder.

Suffering

The opportunity for self-examination often deepens through suffering. Nothing interrupts the ego's imperative to generate happiness and pleasure more than suffering, which also offers a reminder of life's inevitable domination over us. It is the great reminder that life will have its way with us and thus we need one another. The ego attaches easily to the illusion that remaining vigilant and informed and taking a daily regimen of appropriate supplements will surely prevent unwanted suffering. Of course, once we have overcome a bout with pain, it is only too easy to convince ourselves it won't happen again. If suffering prevails, then our denial may gradually be forfeited, paving the way for us to slip into seeing ourselves as life's victim.

The ego often is more comfortable defining itself as conquered by life, especially if it can make a case for why the war lost was no ordinary defeat but rather a cataclysmic victory on behalf of life. The ego would never describe itself as having been part of some superficial skirmish. Maintaining an adversarial relationship to life's suffering will deepen insight neither into ourselves nor into life. Our psychological age is not advanced until we pause, willing to hold curiosity and compassion for what suffering brings to the sufferer.

Suffering can present the pause, allowing us to receive that self we have forsaken in the race of our ambitions and eagerness to achieve. We will need to continue to have a genuine relationship with life if we hope to have any understanding of it. In a real relationship there is ongoing giving and receiving by both parties. Hence, we need to see life as both receiving from us and giving to us. It's only too easy to view suffering as only ripping us off. It will likely take a measure of courage to allow our suffering to create opportunity for an inner truth to get our attention.

In the following quote from Mahatma Gandhi, we can see the resolve necessary in order for suffering to offer testimony to some truth:

> I shall not fear anyone on Earth.
> I shall fear only God.
> I shall not bear ill will toward anyone.
> I shall not submit to injustice from anyone.
> I shall conquer untruth by truth.
> And in resisting untruth, I shall put up with all suffering.

We can allow suffering to open us to deeper levels of self-examination and the possible truths residing there. We can ask, What is this suffering asking of me?

What is the teaching of this suffering? What is possible because of the teaching brought by this suffering? We can follow the lead of

Rumi, who said, "The wound is the place where the light enters you." And then we can ask, What light is attempting to reach me in this suffering? I've noticed that during a recent pause due to foot surgery, my intuition, imagination, and insight have increased measurably. My question is, Am I willing to interrupt the "race of days" in order to access these inner lights that grow dim during the race?

Nothing has the potential to reduce excessive pride like suffering. Through it, we are brought to our creatureliness, our kinship with the animal kingdom. Any sophistication tends to fade into the recesses of our beings, no longer able to prop us up with a propriety that lacks humility and simplicity.

The more we relinquish the conquer-or-be-conquered attitude toward life and let go of an attachment to being clever, we can allow our relationship to ourselves and to life to become more soulful. As John Keats put it, "Do you not see how necessary a World of Pains and troubles is to school an Intelligence and make it a soul?" We can say that schooling an intelligence and making life soulful is mostly about living intimately with ourselves and with life. Emerging into an elder means remaining devoted to giving to life and receiving from it. This will call for letting go of an obsession with being self-reliant, learning to ask for help, and learning to depend upon others.

Dependency

An old definition of the verb *to depend* is "to be because of." In its reign, the ego pretends it is not being because of anything or anyone but itself. If that illusion persists, then the inevitable dependency of old age can be at best intolerable and shameful.

We begin to treat dependency more creatively when we allow our powerlessness to direct us toward asking for help. This constitutes a major opportunity to learn more about being fully human rather than fictitiously fully autonomous.

Learning how to be dependent calls for acquiring at least two important skills. The first skill is being adept at interrupting the story that there is something wrong with us if we need to depend upon someone. The new story has to do with honoring our limits and possessing enough savvy to be able to identify a valuable resource and access that resource.

The second competency is more generic—and quite vital: it is the ability to effectively receive. Very few of us take learning to receive seriously. Our culture certainly does not hold the sanctity of receiving, and receiving can leave us feeling out of control. Giving initiates and defines a dynamic, while receiving is considerably more passive. It is not typical for us to ask, what constitutes an effective receiver?

Since giving and receiving are the two major energies in a rapport-building process, it behooves us to become proficient at both. Here are the principal lessons regarding learning to receive:

- Identifying the old stories we lived in that prohibit receiving.
- Identify what it will take to interrupt the old stories.
- Begin to gradually think of receiving as sacred as giving.
- Begin to see receiving as a way to participate more fully in life and to hold gratitude for what is received.
- Learning to refrain from connecting permission to receive to how much we have given.
- Learning to identify the person who has the ability to meet our need.
- Learning not to personalize it when someone says no to our request.
- Learning to be comfortable expressing sincere gratitude for the help and assistance we receive.

These skills help us to carry our powerlessness and our suffering. We can more readily risk being aware of our powerlessness and suffering because we know how to secure support. We can offer a deeper welcome to our strengths and weaknesses. We can continue to develop our elderhood into old age. We can truly get to know ourselves, especially if we offer compassion to what we discover lives within us.

Compassion

There is an orphan within each of us, someone reaching out in the hope of being received and loved—someone who is desperate to find some place to rest, to be held. The ego longs to forget that someone walked away, leaving us feeling discarded. There lives a quiet anguish blurring our vision and yet longing for some faint luminosity revealing a hidden deservedness to be loved. Yet a self-examining life capable of dethroning the ego must be willing to acknowledge and accept all who reside within. Nothing is more capable of prohibiting and disrupting a life of self-awareness than the impoverishment of compassion.

If we continue to look inside with a gaze laced with disdain, then we likely will find the looking to be intolerable. How easy it is to look at ourselves the way parents, teachers, and clergy have looked at us. We can recall authority figures bent upon observing us with intense scrutiny. Only too often did their inspection insist upon calling us to something better. We may have hungered for a moment or two when we felt we were enough.

But as Carl Rogers teaches us, "The curious paradox is that when I accept myself just as I am, then I can change." Rogers offers us a great reminder of one of the ego's favorite tactics: exercising self-loathing in the name of becoming a better person. When we define ourselves as lowlifes, it does not assure our chances of refining our character. We can easily find ourselves in our later years still hoping to refine our character, rather than having an appreciation for ourselves as wonderful, flawed people. The part of us we turn against typically behaves like a child acting out. We criticize a propensity to be late and continue to be tardy, we find fault with how we eat and continue to eat unhealthy foods, or we denounce some arrogant gesture only to find ourselves caught more frequently in an inflated posture.

In order to bring compassion to some aspect of our character that we denounce, we may need to place that trait into a larger story. A small story might be, "I'm just an inadequate person." When it comes to others, a larger story can be created around remaining curious about a person with an unacceptable quality. Ask yourself, What was I feeling when I reacted harshly? What was I wanting? What was the jagged edge of my reaction asking for? What might I lose if I soften the edge? It's a lot like getting to know someone beyond some single incident or encounter.

Unseating the ego means letting go of an attachment to being special and replacing it with a devotion to honor our uniqueness. Being special implies hierarchy, while honoring uniqueness keeps us self-focused and respecting the inevitable differences between ourselves and others. This self-focusing keeps the responsibility of our personal worth with us, independent of the talents and achievements of others.

A devotion to self-compassion loosens our grip on vanity. Something deeper replaces playing dress-up. We see something more sustainable in ourselves and in others, as Yeats (1994) reveals:

> How many loved your moments of glad grace,
> And loved your beauty with love false or true;
> But one man loved the pilgrim soul in you,
> And loved the sorrows of your changing face.
> (W.B. Yeats, "When You Are Old")

Opening our hearts to the "pilgrim soul" with "the sorrows of a changing face" is a celebration of a life well lived. We confirm that we were always intended to be seekers and allow our souls to be touched by interior and exterior gravity and our faces sculpted, each crease and line confirming the burden and the joy of life.

It is worth staying mindful that the ego abhors being ordinary. From the repulsion of being ordinary, the ego will settle for being either positively special or negatively special. However, the glory of being special will not be forsaken! Hence, we can see declarations of how awful we are as more testimony of the ego's attachment to being special. Compassion calls us to our ordinariness, with our unique strengths, weaknesses, achievements, and failures. And of course, nothing is more ordinary than aging and dying.

Getting to Know Life

As we come to accept our ordinariness, with less striving to be special, we become more acquainted with life. The passion to know the truth about life is the love of wisdom. Life will neither shed its mystery nor its immensity, and it may reveal some faint glimpse of its silhouette. Richard Rohr's statement, "To know truth, you must become the truth," points us toward wisdom. Elders who live with a level of wisdom dare to become the truth.

For example, we can look at what it would mean to know the truth about compassion by becoming the truth of compassion, living the struggle of that truth—which might include being cruel, vindictive, insensitive, and jealous. The path to wisdom begins with becoming a devoted student of compassion. However, living it does not mean attaining it! It means being willing to stumble and fumble with it devotionally.

When we commit to knowing the truth about compassion, ultimately we discover cruelty, revenge, insensitivity, and jealousy. At the point of encountering these darker energies, many will forsake the truth about compassion. The light of compassion is reached by traversing many shadows.

Recently, an old friend told a story about a relative who asked if his son and his son's girlfriend could stay at his home while he was on an extended vacation. He agreed and suggested that the couple could also stay upon his return, for a modest rent. But as the weeks passed, he became aware that his medical condition was diminishing his willingness to cohabitate when he arrived back home. He described the reaction to his change of mind as abrasive and harsh:

> I couldn't believe what I was hearing! Here I was with a serious medical condition and my brother-in-law wanted to interrogate me and imply that my change of plans constituted a breach of contract. I immediately wanted to write him off as a non-caring person whom I could not trust. After some time, I realized he was under a great deal of pressure at work and at home. But that should not mitigate his behavior. I slipped into a self-righteous position, deciding that I don't treat people like that when I'm under pressure.

> Well, it took a bit for me to admit I sometimes come on strong when I'm under pressure. The real truth was that I felt hurt, and it's wasn't the case that my brother-in-law was untrustworthy. I met with him and told him I felt hurt, which made me feel vulnerable. I also said that the truth is that when he responds to me while he's under pressure, I need more of me— more boundaries, more clarity about my own needs, and more voice to represent these. I likely need more boundaries and more clarity about my needs when he's confronting me.

My friend, at sixty-four, had been willing on many occasions to live the truth of compassion. He was simply doing it one more time, wading through anger, distrust, fear, honesty, self-righteousness, vulnerability, and a greater commitment to self-care. He was willing to live in these darker energies rather than make his brother-in-law wrong. I listened with immense respect to an elder who had steadfastly remained in love with wisdom by living in the truth he wished to know. Often the truth we wish to know calls us to live in the truth of who we are.

Through a devotion to know the one traveling the journey, we can come to some understanding of the journey. If we visit New York and we know our experience at the theater, at the Met, at the art galleries in SoHo, and in Chinatown, then we get to know something about New York. So it is with life: if we are willing to become intimately mindful of ourselves—our loving, our success, our defeats, and our losses—then we may come to understand the lived experience we call our life.

When we seek the truth about ourselves and remain committed to offering compassion to what we find about ourselves, we create an intimate connection to life. In that intimacy, as in all intimacies, something wondrous, endearing, and sustainable will be revealed. We come to know the one who loved life dearly, and we come to know the beloved.

This intimacy with life deposes the ego to its rightful dwelling place. Ego imperatives are replaced by soulful gestures: Whom do I serve? What youth am I to steward? What does life ask of me? To whom am I being asked to bring more truth accompanied by compassion? Who is asking for my acknowledgement and my blessing? To whom may I bring comfort? These trans-ego focuses are not motivated by heroism or a need for recognition. They simply reflect the errand of the aging seeker, the maturing elder who can now focus on what it means to get ready to leave.

Getting Ready to Leave

Recently, our astrologer friend updated the influences of planets and the moon upon my current life. At one point on the CD she made, I heard her say, "Well, Paul, it's time to get ready to leave."

That provoked in me the thoughts, *You only tell someone diagnosed with pancreatic cancer that it's time to get ready to leave. Why is she telling me this?*

The reading went on to suggest a perspective of life I had not considered. It takes us twenty to thirty years to get here, twenty to thirty to be here, and twenty to thirty to get ready to leave. I immediately heard the truth of this timetable and was reminded of my denial that I am at the getting-ready-to-leave stage. I decided I wanted to learn more about what getting ready to leave might look like.

One of the great paradoxes is that a fitting preparation for getting ready to leave is actually to be here more, the idea of "more" not meaning attending to some bucket list. In the winter of our life, most of life has been lived. We have more history than future. We can be here more by releasing an attachment to a tenuous future and committing to learning how to remain in the moment. There awaits an abundance of life to be lived in the present moment—probably more life than the ego was willing to handle previously! Being attached to the future allows the ego to indulge in the illusion of being in control by maintaining a focus on its goals and future intentions.

We can only show up in the present. There's no other place to land. The moment is the place where we do life and life does us, with getting done by life not being one of the ego's favorite pastimes. If we have lived devotionally to self-examination accompanied by compassion, then we have grown a large capacity to welcome all we encounter in these moments. These later years no longer find us quaking when hearing a knock on the inner door, and we do not experience our lives as having been stolen.

Theft Prevention

> *When we say we're busy, we're really saying that we're*
> *caught in an emotional complex where our will is*
> *trapped and we're not free to do things we might wish*
> *for ourselves.*
>
> —Thomas Moore, *The Re-Enchantment of*
> *Everyday Life*

We often hear ourselves say things like, "Where did the time go?"
"It seems like the last twenty years went by in a flash!" "It seems just
like yesterday that my kids were starting kindergarten. Now, their
kids are starting school." Busyness steals lives. The rush of life moves
us rapidly into the next moment. Busyness robs us of the present.
But theft prevention means learning to pause, allowing ourselves to
be touched and moved by life. Pausing is great theft prevention and
supports our efforts toward getting ready to leave by helping us be
here more. We claim the moment and feel claimed by the moment.
It is the celebration of a life lived.

Diminished Attachment to Being Witnessed

"Grandpa, watch me roll down the hill." "Watch me hit the ball!" "Watch
me jump over this puddle!" These are examples of my grandchildren
overtly calling for me to witness their varied skills, with the hope of
soliciting my applause—which I inevitably offer. As we become more
self-conscious, we pursue being seen and applauded more subtly.

Our inner voices whisper, "Has anyone noticed how well I'm
doing?" "Does someone see how bright I am?" "What about checking
out how marvelous I am?" I am typically amazed by athletes who,
following some score or excellent act of defense, run about a court
or field with their arms flailing up and down, calling for a more

robust response from the fans. The alleged purpose of this maneuver is to generate more fan-backing of the team. However, I can't help wondering if it is not also a large cry of "See me!" Maybe the athletes are simply doing overtly what we all do more delicately.

Getting ready to leave means releasing the ego's investment in being seen and confirmed by others as OK. Getting ready to leave means reclaiming the privacy of the journey. As the ego relaxes demonstrations of its varied talents, we can settle back into a soulful solitude. It doesn't mean moving into isolation; in fact, we may feel more connected to others than ever. However, it does mean we are less dependent upon impressing others. We feel a deeper personal connection to what we came to give, to receive, and to learn.

It is a deep soulful task to release ourselves from the attachment to being witnessed by others. Peace of mind now comes from the satisfaction of being acquainted with our purpose. We can appreciate the times we weathered the storms that challenged our purpose and the times we were provided with much needed resources.

Life purposes involve learning what we came to offer, learning what we need to learn in order to most effectively make the offering, identifying what mentors and allies are needed to support our delivery, and drawing satisfaction from some level of accomplishment of what we know we needed to do. Also, there is gratitude for those who benefited from our offering as well as those who offered help to make it happen. There can be an endearing calm as we practice releasing others from their assigned task of bringing accolades and commendations to the manifestation of our purpose.

Because of Who We Are

Most of us will live and die anchoring our self-worth in the bay of what we do. Our actions reflect desired achievements and victories offering confirmation of our personal value. Our worthiness is measured by what we deem positive action. In a society where the tangible and quantifiable are treasured, we find it extremely challenging to have even some faint grasp of what it means to have our self-worth reflect who we are and not simply what we do.

When it comes to infants and small children, we have some limited understanding of their value lying somewhere other than in what they do. However, as soon as they are capable of generating behavior we prize, having worth because of who they are typically slips into oblivion. These children are now condemned to endless behavioral demonstrations of their worth.

Elders take on the challenge of moving their personal value out of the area of a job well done to a life well lived, holding an endearing sentiment for who they are. In our obsession with evaluating and measuring, we forget that we are mostly invisible beings. Our beliefs, values, emotions, intentions, longings, and dreams are invisible. Of course, we can come to some fuller appreciation of these invisible realities when they are manifested in action. However, it would be silly to view their success or worth only in terms of expressed action.

We say about someone that he or she has a great heart. We cannot experience the largeness of the heart in particular actions or measure its size like a heart that sits in a dish following an autopsy. However, the description of a large heart might refer to a person's capacity for compassion, generosity, forgiveness, and sensitivity. We can say that such a capacity is some reflection of who they are and what can be deeply valued. But more importantly, the task of valuing ourselves for who we are is deeply personal. The value is mostly a measure of our devotion to deepening our ability to live with more compassion, insight, and generosity. In the final hour, only we will know the extent of our devotional lives.

This new form of valuing, based on devotion, can reflect our motivation and intentions along the way to be truthful, creative, insightful, resolute, and flexible. It may also indicate the depth of gratitude we hold for what life has offered us. Fondly holding these invisibles greatly supports getting ready to leave, as does our last initiation.

Our Last Initiation

Our last initiation will certainly be like the rest. There will be a measure of dying and some important birthing. With a little luck, the aging seeker is less dramatic about what dies, holding more faith in the impending birth. However, elders often share a similar seduction experienced by olders. There is a lure toward the illusion of arrival.

Olders pretend that retiring from a job means they have arrived at a new juncture of entitlement. They now have permission to settle back, play golf, and indulge in an unbridled intake of martinis. Elders, on the other hand, are often bewitched by the thinking that their best efforts at mindful living have been duly exercised. It is now time to settle into the satisfaction of a job well done. However, elders remain on the journey, with life reminding them of a variety of ego attachments still needing attention.

From Arrogance to Humility

Arrogance can best be described as pretending that we possess certain skills or knowledge. It is a denial of our limits. Many of us would have been severely wounded in childhood if we had not pretended or imagined we were much larger than the faultfinding remarks directed at us by authority figures. Arrogance easily moves from being a survival tool to being an ongoing substitute for authentic self-love.

Aging brings about the loss of physical beauty, strength, endurance, and health, as well as the loss of unlived dreams. It is only too easy to compensate for these losses through arrogance. Consequently, even if worked on earlier in life, arrogance can creep up on us in later life.

When this happens, elders are called to revisit the status of humility in our lives.

There are four distinct features of humility:

1. **Acknowledging and accepting our limits**. The ego persists in attempting to have us be bigger than we are. This inflation typically endures failure, frustration, and disillusionment as we attempt to hold command over what is out of our control. Elders are asked to find a peace that accompanies the acceptance of limits. This peace suggests we are part of something larger than us, capable of instructing and guiding us to a deeper understanding of ourselves and of life. Acceptance of our limits tends to generate simplicity. When simplicity ensues, we typically know where we belong, living with less tension, urgency, and dread.

2. **Gratitude for the journey.** Gratitude declares a delight in the challenges and opportunities offered us. We are not caught up in lamenting that we did not have a more elaborate spectacle of a life.

3. **Acceptance of the feeling of helplessness**. Feeling helpless loses its power to diminish us and make us feel inadequate. Accepting helplessness also denotes our participation in a plan much larger than our egos. Feeling helpless is no longer about failure, but rather the ability to surrender to fate. It is simply an indication of our rightful place. We can take solace in knowing where we belong and that more will be revealed.

4. **A desire to serve rather than be served.** Because we are grateful for all that we have been given, we feel called to manifest our gifts in service. We are not waiting to hit the spiritual lottery. Personal fulfillment comes to fruition in the opportunity to make offerings from all that we have been given.

From Conclusions to Curiosity

Elders share with olders the propensity to draw conclusions. On one level, it makes good sense to allow our experience to yield ideological positions we find trustworthy. On the other hand, strong attachments to maintaining conclusions can impede the aging seeker.

Lethargy and mediocrity are the likely results of sitting back in the confines of our conclusions. Rationalizations supporting lethargy vary from "I've done enough," to "It's time to be acknowledged rather than continue to learn," to "I've worked hard and I need to rest," to "I want to feel the satisfaction of a job completed." An important antidote for lethargy is the Hermetic restlessness we examined in Chapter 5. The hope is that we can maintain a restlessness along with a willingness to linger, tempering our efforts at striving. We can hold our unknowing with more compassion as well as with a more supple grip on our conclusions.

An old mentor of mine has published his first book of poetry at eighty-two years old and claims that many of his theological beliefs are undergoing a serious revamping. What a model of the sanctity of Hermetic restlessness!

From Condemnation to Compassion

Elders have come to some understanding that they are called to a unity with others—with all creatures as well as nature itself. The challenge is to continue to integrate an unfolding capacity for compassion. It means letting go of using the shortcomings of others as a temporary psychological scaffolding for our tenuous self-love. It means becoming less self-righteous.

Several questions can be helpful in the opening to deeper compassion: What might I see in the other that is difficult for me to accept about myself? Can I allow myself to remember the mystery of the other's journey and let go of my assessment of who they allegedly are? Can I allow myself to be mindful that the other is wounded, similarly to me? If I need a boundary, separating me from the other, can I employ one without diminishing the other? Can I accept that I am asked to remain a student of compassion to the end of my days?

From Vanity to Authentic Self-Love

Releasing our attachments to a variety of show-pieces remains an ongoing initiation into love. My friend Ci reminds me that we all want to remain attractive. Our hope is that how we look, how we talk, how we think, or what social status we occupy will inevitably elicit pleasurable responses from others.

Certainly, the gift of our aging bodies limits our capacity to lure attention from others. As we have less to put on parade, the more we are called to value ourselves for who we are and not for how we present.

Our preparation to leave points us to the task of diminishing our arrogance, maintaining our curiosity, deepening our capacity for compassion, and holding ourselves with a genuine self-love. The hope is that diminishing these attachments will bring a measure of ease to taking our final breath.

Our Final Opus

> *The end lies concealed in the beginning; but the opposite is also true. The beginning is hidden in all that comes to an end.*
> —Michael Meade

Learning to die is about learning to live; hence, our final opus is to learn more about living and dying. Our nonpermanent life experience is an endless series of something beginning and something ending. In order to learn to die, we may need to change how we think and talk about life, substituting birthing for beginning and dying for ending. It can be very challenging to remain mindful that all births entail a death and all deaths issue in a birth.

The French obstetrician Fredrick Leboyer understood Meade's end lying concealed in the beginning. He reminded us that we get fixated on identifying a fetus emerging from the womb as only constituting a birth, a beginning. He broadened our perspective by suggesting that the fetus is experiencing an ending, a death, a departure from the safest and most supportive environment it will ever know. He recommended that delivery rooms facilitate the death-birth experience of the child by placing the just-born child in warm water and dimming the lights, resembling the environment the child just came from.

A student of death remains mindful of the inextricable link between death and birth. Of course, the challenge might be how mysterious the birth is that follows the death of the body. Given how easy it is to view a child's emerging from the womb as only a birth, death of the body offers a beautiful opportunity for reflection.

We deepen our learning about death as we give ourselves permission to respond robustly and gently to our death-and-dying experiences. The key is to allow ourselves to get close to our losses and feel the sorrow, the anger, and the possible regret over loss. We can allow ourselves to wonder how we need to carry this loss and what the loss may be asking of us.

It can help to identify who can walk with us in our loss. The following poem by Dylan Thomas speaks to the passion of loss:

> Do not go gentle into that good night,
> Old age should burn and rave at close of day;
> Rage, rage against the dying of the light.

> Though wise men at their end know dark is right,
> Because their words had forked no lightning they
> Do not go gentle into that good night.
>
> Good men, the last wave by, crying how bright
> Their frail deeds might have danced in a green bay,
> Rage, rage against the dying of the light.
>
> Wild men who caught and sang the sun in flight,
> And learn, too late, they grieved it on its way,
> Do not go gentle into that good night.
>
> Grave men, near death, who see with blinding sight
> Blind eyes could blaze like meteors and be gay,
> Rage, rage against the dying of the light.
>
> And you, my father, there on that sad height,
> Curse, bless, me now with your fierce tears, I pray.
> Do not go gentle into that good night.
> Rage, rage against the dying of the light.
> (Dylan Thomas, "Do Not Go Gentle into That Good Night")

Thomas offers us the passion of one who loves the light—"Rage, rage against the dying of the light." How fitting it is to rage in response to what is loved and lost! It would be too easy to simply view Thomas's position as simply a protest of death, rather than a prayer in honor of a life deeply loved and revered.

The next poem, by Emily Dickinson, portrays more surrender and acceptance of loss:

> Because I could not stop for Death—
> He kindly stopped for me—
> The Carriage held but just Ourselves—
> And Immortality.

We slowly drove—he knew no haste
And I had put away
My labor and my leisure too,
For His Civility—

We passed the School, where Children strove
At Recess—in the Ring—
We passed the Fields of Gazing Grain—
We passed the Setting Sun—

Or rather—He passed Us—
The Dews grew quivering and Chill—
For only Gossamer, my Gown—
My Tippet—only Tulle—

We paused before a House that seemed
A Swelling of the Ground—
The Roof was scarcely visible—
The Cornice—in the ground—

Since then— 'tis centuries— and yet
Feels shorter than the Day
I first surmised the Horses' Heads
Were toward Eternity—
(Emily Dickinson, "Because I could not stop for Death")

Biophilia

There is no better way to get ready to leave than to deepen our love of life, *biophilia*. It is an intense involvement with life that leaves us with a deep feeling of having fully lived, not holding back. As we honor a beginner's heart and mind, there is so much to learn and so much to do—and there are so many opportunities to be generous and grateful.

Even as we relax into stillness, there is so much. We are reminded of how it feels to let go of the rush of life, surrendering to the rhythm of the breath, one inhale ushering in an exhale and back again. We can feel welcomed by the quiet of life. The emptiness is filled with gratitude for having been given the journey. When treating life as the beloved, our love is consummated in some measure of wisdom.

The question is not, what is wisdom? Rather, the question is, how is wisdom? This question captures the ongoing, active involvement of wisdom. We can say that wisdom is the child born from the love affair we have with life. It's an emotionally intimate affair, one in which we want to feel, know, and receive our beloved in as many ways as possible. It is the willingness to unearth the truth within, holding and speaking that truth with increased compassion that reveals the care we hold for what we have been shown. Wisdom is the act of pausing and listening, believing we will be more deeply informed, holding the faith that life wants to be known by us.

Unlike knowledge, wisdom is not compiled under certain categories and headings. Wisdom is involvement moved by curiosity and wonder. It is believing that the present situation is pregnant with instruction and holds a hunger to be duly instructed. Wisdom is knowing when to rest, allowing our experience to incubate. Wisdom is the act of allowing ourselves to fall into the embrace of life. We then come to know the act of unity we call home.

A Blessing for the Aging Seeker

Remember yourself as the courageous one, carrying yourself through many dis-illusions. You bore the loss of your way, embraced doubt that left you quivering in the arms of ambiguity, no longer attached to a contrived certainty.

When there was nowhere outside to look, you looked within and found illusions of permanence, illusions of power, and the illusion of absolute self-reliance. You found yourself face-to-face with an ego demanding its dominion.

You dared to dethrone the ego monarch with no real understanding of where inner authority would come from. Now, you were asked to trust feeling powerless, allowing acts of triumph to fade back to younger days.

With an ego finding its proper place within the inner kingdom, a sacred agency, a new governing body emerged: your devotion to remaining self-examining. You were now willing to become acquainted and intimate with that reflection of life most available to you: your soul.

The years failed to steal life from you! As you embraced impermanence, you received the kiss of life as you stood in the moment, the only place where life truly thrives. In this intimate connection, attachments to vengeance found conclusion in a new forgiveness.

Now, as an elder, not as an older, you accept the soul's mandate to get ready to leave. You have learned to let go of an unquenchable thirst to be witnessed and applauded. You now know that being willing to learn to die taught you how to live, with every death ushering in a birth.

You have rightly come to the place of the deep knowing where your essential worth resides in your Being, not your doing. This is the house of your devotion to truth and compassion, where your sense of wonder lives with your commitment to remain a beginner.

Your elderhood lives in your kinship to all things. As a seeker you have found home in such intimacy. You are free to honor the great love affair you called "my life." "Rage, rage against the dying of the light. Do not go gently into that good night."

Your body leaves you now. You still dream the old dream. You see your friend with eyes no longer gripped by difference, better or worse. The old dream lets you see aging and dying as the common destiny. You are not alone.

References

Becker, Ernest. 1975. *Escape from Evil*. New York: Free Press.

Dickinson, Emily. 1960. *The Complete Poems of Emily Dickinson*. Boston: Little, Brown.

Frankl, Viktor E. 2006. *Man's Search for Meaning*. Boston: Beacon Press.

Harper, Ralph. 1965. *The Seventh Solitude: Man's Isolation in Kierkegaard, Dostoevsky, and Nietzsche*. Baltimore: Johns Hopkins Press.

Hollis, James. 2005. *Finding Meaning in the Second Half of Life*. New York: Gotham.

Huxley, Aldous. 1942. *The Art of Seeing*. New York: Harper.

Johnson, Robert, and Jerry M. Ruhl. 2000. *Contentment: A Way to True Happiness*. San Francisco: HarperSanFrancisco.

Julian of Norwich. 2009. *The Complete Julian of Norwich*. Translated by Father John-Julian. Brewster, MA: Paraclete Press.

Jung, Carl G. 1997. *The Seminars: Volume Two, Part I*. Princeton, NJ: Princeton University Press.

Keats, John. 1958. *The Letters of John Keats, 1814–1821.* Cambridge, MA: Harvard University Press.

Kornfield, Jack. 1993. *A Path with Heart: A Guide Through the Perils and Promises of Spiritual Life.* New York: Bantam Books.

Lamb, Charles. 2011. "A Chapter on Ears." In *The Essays of Elia.* New York: Barnes & Noble.

Levine, Peter. 1997. *Waking the Tiger: Healing Trauma—The Innate Capacity to Transform Overwhelming Experiences.* Berkeley, CA: North Atlantic Books.

———. 2010. *In an Unspoken Voice: How the Body Releases Trauma and Restores Goodness.* Berkeley, CA: North Atlantic Books.

Lewis, C.S. 1943. *The Screwtape Letters.* New York: Macmillan.

López-Pedraza, Rafael. 1977. *Hermes and His Children.* Zurich: Spring.

May, Rollo. 1994. *The Courage to Create.* New York: W.W. Norton.

Meade, Michael. 2012. *Why the World Doesn't End: Tales of Renewal in Times of Loss.* Seattle: Greenfire Press.

Miller, Alice. 1981. *Prisoners of Childhood: The Drama of the Gifted Child and the Search for the True Self.* New York: Basic Books.

Moore, Thomas. 1996. *The Re-Enchantment of Everyday Life.* New York: HarperCollins.

———. 2014. *A Religion of One's Own: A Guide to Creating a Personal Spirituality in a Secular World.* New York: Gotham Books.

Nouwen, Henri J.M. 1988. *The Road to Daybreak: A Spiritual Journey.*
New York: Doubleday.

O'Donohue, John. 2008. *To Bless the Space Between Us: A Book of Blessings.* New York: Doubleday.

Peck, M. Scott. 1998. *The Different Drum: Community-Making and Peace.* 2nd. ed. New York: Touchstone.

Rilke, Rainer M., Franz Xavier Kappus, and Stephen Mitchell. 1984. *Letters to a Young Poet.* New York: Random House.

Robinson, John C. 1995. *Death of a Hero, Birth of the Soul: Answering the Call of Midlife.* Sacramento: Tzedakah.

Rohr, Richard. 2005. *What the Mystics Know: Seven Pathways to Your Deeper Self.* New York: Disinformation.

Rogers, Carl. 1980. *A Way of Being.* Boston: Houghton Mifflin.

Yeats, W.B. 1994. *The Collected Poems of W.B. Yeats.* London: Wordsworth Editions Limited.